PSALMS ANEW

In Inclusive Language

PSALMS ANEW

In Inclusive Language

**Nancy Schreck, OSF, and
Maureen Leach, OSF**

Saint Mary's Press
Christian Brothers Publications
Winona, Minnesota

To all who,
by their vision and labor,
helped to give birth to this project,
especially our Franciscan sisters.

The publishing team for this publication included Carl Koch, FSC, editor; Miriam Frost, manuscript editor; Lynn Dahdal, production editor; and Carolyn Thomas, designer and calligrapher.

Printed in the United States of America

Printing—sixth fifth fourth third
        1993 92 91 90 89 88 87

ISBN 0-88489-174-7

PREFACE

Psalms Anew: In Inclusive Language

salms *Anew has been created for those who love to pray the Psalms alone or in communal prayer and are committed to the use of inclusive language. These Psalms remain as faithful as possible to the* original text so as to guard the authenticity of the Psalms while at the same time freeing them from their patriarchal bias.

We offer thanks to many friends along the way who by their encouragement and supportive service have made this book a reality.

Nancy Schreck, OSF • Berkeley, California

Maureen Leach, OSF • Mission, Texas

CONTENTS

 Four-Week Psalter for Morning and Evening Prayer
Benedictus
Magnificat
Doxology

PSALMS

S U N D A Y

1   Psalm 63:1–8
    Daniel 3:57–88
    Psalm 149

    Psalm 110:1–5,7
    Psalm 114
    Revelation 19:1–2,5–8
    (Lent: 1 Peter 2:21–24)

2   Psalm 118
    Daniel 3:52–57
    Psalm 150

    Psalm 110:1–5,7
    Psalm 115
    Revelation 19:1–2,5–8
    (Lent: 1 Peter 2:21–24)

3   Psalm 93
    Daniel 3:57–88
    Psalm 148

    Psalm 110:1–5,7
    Psalm 111
    Revelation 19:1–2,5–8
    (Lent: 1 Peter 2:21–24)

4   Psalm 118
    Daniel 3:52–57
    Psalm 150

    Psalm 110:1–5,7
    Psalm 112
    Revelation 19:1–2,5–8
    (Lent: 1 Peter 2:21–24)

M O N D A Y

1   Psalm 5:1–12
    1 Chronicles 29:10–13
    Psalm 29

    Psalm 11
    Psalm 15
    Ephesians 1:3–10

2   Psalm 42
    Ecclesiasticus (Sirach)
    36:1–5,10–13
    Psalm 19:1–7

    Psalm 45:1–9
    Psalm 45:10–17
    Ephesians 1:3–10

3   Psalm 84
    Isaiah 2:2–5
    Psalm 96

    Psalm 123
    Psalm 124
    Ephesians 1:3–10

4   Psalm 90
    Isaiah 42:10–16
    Psalm 135:1–12

    Psalm 136:1–9
    Psalm 136:10–26
    Ephesians 1:3–10

TUESDAY

1 Psalm 24
Tobit 13:1–8
Psalm 33

Psalm 20
Psalm 21:1–7,13
Revelation 4:11; 5:9,10,12

2 Psalm 43
Isaiah 38:10–14,16–20
Psalm 65

Psalm 49:1–13
Psalm 49:14–21
Revelation 4:11; 5:9,10,12

3 Psalm 85
Isaiah 26:1–4,7–9,12
Psalm 67

Psalm 125
Psalm 131
Revelation 4:11; 5:9,10,12

4 Psalm 101
Daniel 3:26,27,29–41
Psalm 144:1–10

Psalm 137:1–6
Psalm 138
Revelation 4:11; 5:9,10,12

WEDNESDAY

1 Psalm 36
Judith 16:2–3a,13–15
Psalm 47

Psalm 27:1–6
Psalm 27:7–14
Colossians 1:11–20

2 Psalm 77
1 Samuel 2:1–10
Psalm 97

Psalm 62
Psalm 67
Colossians 1:11–20

3 Psalm 86
Isaiah 33:13–16
Psalm 98

Psalm 126
Psalm 127
Colossians 1:11–20

4 Psalm 108
Isaiah 61:10—62:5
Psalm 146

Psalm 139:1–12
Psalm 139:13–18,23
Colossians 1:11–20

T H U R S D A Y   F R I D A Y

1 Psalm 57
   Jeremiah 31:10–14
   Psalm 48

   Psalm 30
   Psalm 32
   Revelation 11:17–18; 12:10–12

2 Psalm 80
   Isaiah 12:1–6
   Psalm 81

   Psalm 72:1–11
   Psalm 72:12–19
   Revelation 11:17–18; 12:10–12

3 Psalm 87
   Isaiah 40:10–17
   Psalm 99

   Psalm 132:1–10
   Psalm 132:11–18
   Revelation 11:17–18; 12:10–12

4 Psalm 143:1–11
   Isaiah 66:10–14a
   Psalm 147:1–11

   Psalm 144:1–8
   Psalm 144:9–15
   Revelation 11:17–18; 12:10–12

1 Psalm 51
   Isaiah 45:15–25
   Psalm 100

   Psalm 41
   Psalm 46
   Revelation 15:3–4

2 Psalm 51
   Habakkuk 3:2–4,13a,15–19
   Psalm 147:12–20

   Psalm 116:1–9
   Psalm 121
   Revelation 15:3–4

3 Psalm 51
   Jeremiah 14:17–21
   Psalm 100

   Psalm 135:1–12
   Psalm 135:13–21
   Revelation 15:3–4

4 Psalm 51
   Tobit 13:8–11,13,15
   Psalm 147:12–20

   Psalm 145:1–13
   Psalm 145:14–21
   Revelation 15:3–4

SATURDAY

1 Psalm 119:145–152
Exodus 15:1–4,8–13,17–18
Psalm 117

Psalm 119:105–112
Psalm 16
Philippians 2:6–11

2 Psalm 92
Deuteronomy 32:1–12
Psalm 8

Psalm 113
Psalm 116:10–19
Philippians 2:6–11

3 Psalm 119:145–152
Wisdom 9:1–6,9–11
Psalm 117

Psalm 122
Psalm 130
Philippians 2:6–11

4 Psalm 92
Ezekiel 36:24–28
Psalm 8

Psalm 141:1–9
Psalm 142
Philippians 2:6–11

Blessed are you, God of Israel,
because you have visited and ransomed your people.

You raised up a horn of saving strength for us
in the house of David your servant,
as you promised through the mouths of your holy ones,
the prophets of ancient times.

Salvation from our enemies and from the hands of all our foes.
You dealt mercifully with our ancestors
and remembered the holy covenant you made:

the oath you swore to Abraham and Sarah you would grant us—
that rid of fear and delivered from the enemy,
we should serve you devoutly
and through all our days be holy in your sight.

And you, O child, you shall be called the prophet of the Most High,
for you shall go ahead to prepare a straight path for the Most High,
giving the people knowledge of salvation in freedom from their sins.

All this is the work of the kindness of our God,
the dayspring who shall visit us in mercy
to shine on those who sit in darkness and the shadow of death,
to guide our feet into the way of peace.

MAGNIFICAT

My being proclaims your greatness,
and my spirit finds joy in you, God my Savior.

For you have looked upon me, your servant, in my lowliness;
all ages to come shall call me blessed.

God, you who are mighty, have done great things for me.
Holy is your name.

Your mercy is from age to age toward those who fear you.

You have shown might with your arm
and confused the proud in their inmost thoughts.

You have deposed the mighty from their thrones
and raised the lowly to high places.

The hungry you have given every good thing
while the rich you have sent away empty.

You have upheld Israel your servant, ever mindful of your mercy—

even as you promised our ancestors;
promised Abraham, Sarah, and their descendants forever.

DOXOLOGY

Glory be to God our Creator,
to Jesus the Christ,
and to the Holy Spirit who dwells in our midst,
both now and forever. Amen.

PSALM 1

True Happiness

1 **O**h, the joys of those
who walk not after the advice of the wicked,
nor stand in the path of sinners,
nor sit in the seat of scoffers,
2 but delight in the law of Yahweh
and ponder it day and night.
3 They are like trees planted by streams of water
that yield fruit in due season,
whose leaves do not wither;
and everything they do prospers.
4 The ungodly are not so
but are like chaff which the wind blows away.
5 Therefore, they cannot stand firm when Judgment comes,
nor shall sinners find a place in the assembly of the righteous.
6 For God knows the way of the just,
but the way of the ungodly ends in ruin.

PSALM 2

The Reign of the Messiah

1 **W**hy this tumult among nations,
among peoples this useless murmuring?
2 The rulers of the earth arise
and plot against Yahweh and the Anointed.
3 "Come, let us break their chains!
Come, let us cast off their yoke!"
4 The One who sits in the heavens laughs;
Yahweh derides them.
5 Then God will speak to them in anger
and in rage will strike them with terror.

6 "It is I who have set up my ruler
on Zion, my holy mountain."

7 I will proclaim the decree of God.
God said to me: "You are mine.
It is I who have begotten you this day.

8 Ask and I shall bequeath you the nations,
make the ends of the earth in your possession.

9 With a rod of iron you will break them,
shatter them like a potter's jar."

10 Now, O leaders, understand;
take warning, rulers of the earth.

11 Serve God with awe and trembling,
paying homage,

12 lest God be angry and you perish;
for God's anger will suddenly blaze.
Blessed are they who put their trust in God.

P S A L M   3

Trust in God in Time of Danger

1 Yahweh, more and more people are turning against me,
more and more rebelling against me,

2 more and more saying about me,
"There is no help for you in your God."

3 But you, Yahweh, my encircling shield,
my glory, you help me lift up my head.

4 Loudly I cry to Yahweh,
who answers me from the holy mountain.

5 Now I can lie down and sleep
and then awake, for Yahweh sustains me;

6 I am not afraid of those tens of thousands
posted against me wherever I turn.

7 Rise, Yahweh!
Save me, my God!
You crack the cheekbones of my enemies,
You break the teeth of the wicked.
8 From you, Yahweh, deliverance.
On your people, blessing!

P S A L M 4

Evening Prayer for Help

1 Answer me when I call, God, my defender!
When I was in trouble, you came to my help.
Be kind to me now; hear my prayer!
2 How long will you people insult me?
How long will you love what is worthless
and seek what is false?
3 Remember that Yahweh has chosen me
and hears me when I call.
4 Tremble, and stop your sinning;
think deeply about this, alone and silent in your rooms.
5 Offer the right sacrifices to the Holy One
and put your trust in God.
6 There are many who say, "How we wish to receive a blessing!"
Look on us with kindness, Yahweh!
7 The joy that you give me is much greater
than the joy of those who have an abundance of grain and wine.
8 As soon as I lie down, I peacefully go to sleep;
you alone, my Strength, keep me perfectly safe.

Prayer for Divine Help

1 **H**arken to my words, O God,
   attend to my musing.
2 Heed my call for help,
   to you I pray.
3 In the morning you hear my voice;
   at dawn I will make ready and watch for you.
4 For you, O God, delight not in wickedness;
   no one who is evil remains with you.
5 The arrogant may not stand in your sight;
   you hate all who do futile things.
6 You destroy all who speak falsehood;
   the bloodthirsty and the deceitful you detest.
7 But I, through your abundant kindness,
   will enter your house;
   I will worship at your holy Temple
   in fear of you.
8 Because of my enemies, guide me in your justice;
   make straight your way before me.
9 For in their mouths there is no truth;
   their hearts teem with treacheries.
   Their throats are open graves;
   they flatter with their tongues.
10 Hold them guilty, O God;
   let them fall by their own devices.
   For their many sins, cast them out,
   for they have rebelled against you.
11 But let all who take refuge in you
   be glad and rejoice forever.
12 Protect them, O God, bless the just;
   surround them like a shield
   and crown them with your favor.

PSALM 6

Prayer in Time of Distress

1 **Y**ahweh, rebuke me not in your anger,
   nor chasten me in your wrath.
2 Be gracious to me, for I am weak;
   heal me, for my heart is troubled.
3 My soul also is sorely troubled.
4 Turn and save my life;
   deliver me for the sake of your steadfast love,
5 for in death you are not remembered.
   In Sheol who can sing your praise?
6 I am weary with my moaning;
   every night I flood my bed with tears,
   I drench my couch with my weeping.
7 My eyes waste away because of grief;
   I grow weak because of my foes.
8 Leave me, all you worshipers of idols,
   for Yahweh has heard the sound of my weeping.
9 Yahweh has heard my supplication
   and accepts my prayer.
10 All my enemies shall be ashamed and greatly troubled;
   they shall turn back and be put to shame in a moment.

PSALM 7

Appeal to God's Justice

1 **G**od, I take refuge in you.
   From my pursuer save and deliver me
2 lest my enemy tear me to pieces like a lion
   and drag me off with no one to rescue me.
3 God, if my hands have done wrong,
4 if I have paid back evil for good—
   I who saved my unjust oppressor—

5 then let my enemy chase me, seize me,
   trample my life to the ground,
   and toss my soul in the dust.

6 O God of Justice, rise up in your fury;
   rise against the attacks of my foes.
   My God, awake! You will give them judgment.

7 Let all the nations gather round you;
   take your seat on high above them.

8 (You are judge of the peoples.)
   Judge me, O God, according to my righteousness
   and according to the integrity of my heart.

9 Put an end to the evil of the wicked!
   Make the just stand firm,
   you who test mind and heart,
   O just God!

10 God is the shield that protects me,
   who saves the good of heart.

11 God is a just judge,
   slow to wrath,
   but is enraged

12 by those who will not repent.
   God will sharpen the sword,
   brace the bow and take aim.

13 For the wicked, God prepares deadly weapons,
   and barbs arrows with fire.

14 Here is one who is brimming with malice,
   who conceives evil and brings forth lies;

15 One who digs a pit, digs it deep;
   and then falls into the trap.

16 O evildoer, your malice will recoil on you;
   on your own head your violence will fall.

17 I will thank Yahweh for justice;
   I will sing to the Most High.

The Majesty of God and the Dignity of Humanity

1 O God, our God,
    how glorious is your name over all the earth!
    Your glory is praised in the heavens.
2 Out of the mouths of children and babes
    you have fashioned praise because of your foes,
    to silence the enemy and the rebellious.
3 When I look at your heavens, the work of your hands,
    the moon and the stars which you created—
4 who are we that you should be mindful of us,
    that you should care for us?
5 You have made us little less than the gods
    and crowned us with glory and honor.
6 You have given us rule over the works of your hands,
    putting all things under our feet:
7 all sheep and oxen,
    yes, and the beasts of the field;
8 the birds of the air, the fishes of the sea,
    and whatever swims the paths of the seas.
9 God, our God,
    how glorious is your name over all the earth!

God Saves the Humble

1 I will praise you, Yahweh, with my whole heart;
    I will proclaim your wonderful works.
2 I will be glad and rejoice in you;
    I will sing praise to your name, Most High.
3 When my enemies are turned back,
    they stumble and perish before you,

4 for you have maintained my right and upheld my cause.
  You occupy the throne, a righteous judge.
5 You have rebuked the nations and destroyed the wicked.
  You blotted out their name forever and ever.
6 The enemy has vanished in everlasting ruin.
  You have overthrown the cities,
  even the memory of them has perished.
7 But you abide forever
  and have established a throne for judging.
8 You will judge the world in righteousness,
  ministering justice to peoples with equity.
9 So shall you be a stronghold for the oppressed,
  a stronghold in troubled times.
10 Thus shall those who know your name trust in you,
  for you have not forsaken those who sought you.
11 Sing praise to Yahweh, who dwells in Zion;
  declare God's works among the people.
12 For Yahweh, who avenges blood, remembers them;
  Yahweh does not forget the cry of the afflicted.
13 Be gracious to me, Yahweh;
  see what I suffer from those who hate me,
  O you who lift me up from the gates of death,
14 that I may recount all your praises,
  that in the gates of the city of Zion
  I may rejoice in your deliverance.
15 The nations have sunk into the pit that they made;
  Their own feet have been caught in the net that they hid.
16 In passing sentence, Yahweh is manifest;
  the wicked are trapped by the work of their own hands.
17 The wicked shall depart to Sheol,
  all those who forget God.
18 For the needy shall not always be forgotten,
  nor the hope of the poor be lost forever.
19 Arise, Yahweh! let not the sinner prevail;
  let the nations be judged before you.
20 Put them in fear, O God!
  Let the nations know that they are but human.

Prayer for Help against Oppressors

1 **W**hy do you stand aloof, O God?
Why do you hide yourself in times of trouble?

2 In arrogance the wicked oppress the poor
who are caught in the schemes
that the wicked have devised.

3 For the wicked boast of their hearts' desires,
and those greedy for gain curse and renounce you.

4 The wicked do not seek you, because of their pride;
All their thoughts are, "There is no God."

5 The ways of the wicked prosper at all times;
your judgments are on high, out of their sight.
As for all their foes, they scorn them.

6 They think in their hearts, "We shall not be moved;
throughout all generations we shall not meet adversity."

7 Their mouths are filled with cursing, deceit, and oppression;
under their tongues are mischief and fraud.

8 They lurk in ambush in the villages;
in hiding places they murder the innocent;
their eyes stealthily watch for the helpless.

9 They lie in wait that they may seize the poor;
they catch the afflicted and draw them into their net.

10 The helpless are crushed, sink down,
and fall by their might.

11 They think in their hearts,
"God forgets, hides, and never will see it."

12 Arise, Yahweh! O God, lift up your hand!
Forget not the afflicted!

13 Why do the wicked renounce you, God,
and say in their hearts, "You will not call to account"?

14 You do see; yes, you behold misery and sorrow,
taking them into your hands.
The helpless commit themselves to you,
you have been the helper of the orphan.

15 Break the strength of the wicked and evildoer;
   seek out wickedness till you find none.
16 Yahweh rules forever and ever;
   the nations shall perish from the land.
17 Yahweh, you will hear the desire of the afflicted;
   you will strengthen their hearts; you will incline your ear
18 to do justice to the orphan and the oppressed,
   so that those born of earth may strike terror no more.

P S A L M   1 1

The Confidence of the Virtuous

1 In Yahweh I take shelter.
   How can you say to me,
   "Bird, fly back to your mountain!
2 See how the wicked are bending their bows
   and fitting their arrows to the string,
   ready to shoot the upright from the shadows.
3 When foundations fall to ruin,
   what can the virtuous do?"
4 Yahweh is in the holy Temple—
   Yahweh whose throne is in heaven,
   whose eyes look down at the world,
   whose searching gaze scans all.
5 Yahweh tests the just and the wicked;
   God hates the lover of violence,
6 sending fire and brimstone on the wicked.
   A scorching wind is their lot.
7 Yahweh is just and loves justice,
   the upright shall see God's face.

P S A L M   1 2

Prayer against Evil Tongues

1 **H**elp, O Yahweh! for no one now is devout;
   faithfulness has vanished from among the people.
2 People speak falsehood to their neighbor;
   with smooth lips and double heart they speak.
3 May Yahweh destroy all smooth lips,
   every boastful tongue—
4 those who say, "We are strong with our tongues;
   our lips are our own. Who rules over us?"
5 "Because they rob the afflicted, and the needy sigh,
   now will I arise," says Yahweh;
   "I will grant safety to those who long for it."
6 The promises of Yahweh are sure,
   like tried silver, freed from dross, sevenfold refined.
7 You will guard us and preserve us always
   from this generation,
8 while about us the wicked strut,
   and in high places are the basest of people.

P S A L M   1 3

A Confident Appeal

1 **H**ow long, O God? Will you forget me forever?
   How long will you hide your face from me?
2 How long must I bear pain in my soul,
   and have sorrow in my heart all the day?
   How long shall my enemy have the upper hand over me?
3 Consider and answer me, O God:
   give light to my eyes, lest I sleep in death—
4 lest my enemy say, "I have prevailed,"
   and my foes rejoice because I am shaken.

5 But I have trusted in your steadfast love;
   my heart shall rejoice in your salvation.
6 I will sing to you, O God,
   because you have dealt bountifully with me.

P S A L M 1 4

The Wickedness of Humanity

1 **F**ools say to themselves,
   "God doesn't matter!"
   Such are corrupt; they have done terrible deeds.
   There is not one who does what is right.
2 Yahweh looks down from heaven
   to see if there are any who are wise,
   any who worship God.
3 But they have all gone astray;
   they are all equally bad.
   Not one of them does what is right,
   not a single one.
4 "Don't they know?" asks Yahweh.
   "Are all these evildoers ignorant?
   They who eat up my people just as they eat bread
   and do not pray to me?"
5 But they will become terrified
   because God is with those who are just.
6 They make fun of the plans of the helpless
   who trust in Yahweh.
7 How I pray that salvation will come to Israel from Zion!
   When Yahweh makes the faithful prosperous again,
   Jacob and Rachel's descendants will be happy;
   the people of Israel will be glad.

The Guests of Yahweh

1 **Y**ahweh, who has the right to enter your tent,
or to live on your holy mountain?
2 Those whose way of life is blameless,
who always do what is right,
who speak the truth from their heart,
3 whose tongue is not used for slander,
who do no wrong to friends,
cast no discredit on neighbors,
4 who look with contempt on the reprobate,
but honor those who fear you,
who stand by a pledge at all cost,
5 who do not ask interest on loans,
and cannot be bribed to exploit the innocent.
If they do all this, nothing can ever shake them.

P S A L M   1 6

A Prayer of Confidence

1 **P**rotect me, God, because I come to you for safety.
2 I say, "You are my God;
all the good things I have come from you."
3 How wonderful are your faithful people!
My greatest pleasure is to be with them.
4 Those who rush to other gods
bring many troubles on themselves.
I will not take part in their sacrifices;
I will not worship their gods.
5 You, Yahweh, are all I have,
and you give me all I need: my life is in your hands.

6 How wonderful are your gifts to me;
how good they are!

7 I praise Yahweh, who guides me,
and in the night my conscience teaches me.

8 I am always aware of your presence;
you are near, and nothing can shake me.

9 And so I am full of happiness and joy,
and I always feel secure.

10 Because you will not allow me
to go to the world of the dead;
you will not abandon to the depths below
the one you love.

11 You will show me the path that leads to life;
your presence fills me with joy,
and your help brings pleasure forever.

P S A L M   1 7

Appeal of an Upright Person

1 **Y**ahweh, hear a cause that is just;
listen to my pleading.
Incline your ear to my prayer:
no lie is on my lips.

2 From you may my judgment come forth.
Your eyes search out the truth.

3 You study my heart; you visit me by night.
You test me and find no wrong.

4 My words are not sinful as are the words of others.
I kept from violence because of your word.

5 I kept my feet firmly in your paths;
there was no stumbling in my steps.

6 I am here and I call; you will hear me, O God.
Turn your ear to me; hear my words.

7 Demonstrate your great love,
   you whose right hand saves your friends
   from those who rebel against them.
8 Guard me as the apple of your eye.
   Hide me in the shadow of your wings
9 from the savage attacks of the wicked.
   My enemies surround me with vicious intent.
10 They have closed their cruel hearts,
   with their mouths they speak proudly.
11 They advance against me, and now they encircle me.
   Their eyes are watching to throw me to the ground
12 as though they were lions ready to spring,
   like a great lion crouched in cover.
13 Yahweh, arise! Confront them; overthrow them!
   Let your sword rescue me from the wicked;
14 let your hand deliver me from those
   whose reward is in this present life.
15 As for me, in my justice, I shall see your face,
   and be filled, when I awake, with the sight of your glory.

P S A L M   1 8

Thanksgiving for Help in Victory

1 I love you, God, my strength.
2 You are my rock, my fortress, and my deliverer;
   my God, my protector in whom I take refuge, my shield,
   and the horn of my salvation, my stronghold.
3 I call upon you, who are worthy to be praised,
   and I am saved from my enemies.
4 The cords of death encompassed me,
   the destroying floods overwhelmed me.

5 The cords of Sheol entangled me,
   the snares of death confronted me.

6 In my distress I called upon you;
   to you, my God, I cried for help.
   From your Temple you heard my voice,
   and my cry to you reached your ears.

7 Then the earth swayed and rocked;
   the mountains trembled and quaked
   because you were angry.

8 Smoke went up from your nostrils,
   and devouring fire from your mouth;
   glowing coals flamed forth.

9 You bowed the heavens and came down;
   thick darkness was under your feet.

10 You rode on a cherub and flew;
   you came swiftly upon the wings of the wind.

11 You made darkness a covering,
   your canopy, thick clouds dark with water.

12 From the lightning of your presence
   there broke through your clouds hailstones and coals of fire.

13 You thundered in the heavens,
   you, the Most High, shouting.

14 And you sent out your arrows and scattered them;
   you flashed forth lightning and routed them.

15 Then the bed of the sea appeared
   and the foundations of the world were laid bare
   at your rebuke, O God,
   at the blast of the breath of your nostrils.

16 You reached from on high and you grasped me;
   you drew me out of deep waters.

17 You delivered me from my strong enemy,
   and from those who hated me;
   for they were too mighty for me.

18 They came upon me when I was down,
   but you were my support.

19 You brought me forth into a broad place;
   you delivered me because you love me.

20 You, God, reward me according to my righteousness;
according to the cleanness of my hands,
you have given me my due.
21 For I have kept your ways,
and I have not wickedly departed from you, my God.
22 For all your ways were before me,
and your statutes I did not reject.
23 I was blameless before you,
and I kept myself from guilt.
24 Therefore you respond to me
according to my righteousness,
according to the cleanness of my hands in your sight.
25 With the loyal you show yourself loyal;
with the blameless you show yourself blameless.
26 With the pure you show yourself pure,
and with the crooked you show yourself astute.
27 For you deliver a humble people,
but the haughty eyes you bring down.
28 Yes, you light my lamp;
my God, you lighten my darkness.
29 Yes, by you I can run against an armed band,
and by you I can leap over a wall.
30 God, your way is perfect;
your promise proves true;
you are a shield
for all those who take refuge in you.
31 For who is God, but you?
And who is a rock, except our God?—
32 the God who girded me with strength
and made my way safe,
33 who made my feet like hinds' feet
and set me secure on the heights,
34 who trained my hands
so that my arms can bend a bronze bow.
35 You have given me the shield of your salvation;
your right hand supported me, and your help made me great.

36 You gave a wide place for my steps under me,
and my feet did not slip.

37 I pursued my enemies and overtook them,
and did not turn back till they were crushed.

38 I left them shattered, not able to rise;
they fell under my feet.

39 For you girded me with strength for the battle;
you made my assailants sink under me.

40 You made my enemies turn their backs to me,
and those who hated me you destroyed.

41 They cried for help, but there was none to save;
they cried to God, but God did not answer them.

42 I ground them fine as dust before the wind;
I cast them out like the dirt of the streets.

43 You delivered me from strife with the peoples.
You made me the head of the nations;
people whom I had not known served me.

44 As soon as they heard of me they obeyed me;
foreigners came cringing to me.

45 Foreigners lost heart
and came trembling out of their security.

46 God lives! Blessed be my rock,
exalted be the God of my salvation—

47 the God who gave me vengeance,
and subdued peoples under me;

48 who delivered me from my enemies.
Yes, you exalted me above my adversaries;
you delivered me from people of violence.

49 For this I will extol you, O God, among the nations,
and sing praise to your name.

50 Great triumph you give to your leader,
and show steadfast love to your anointed,
to David and his descendants forever.

Praise to God, Creator and Lawgiver

1 The heavens proclaim your glory, O God,
   and the firmament shows forth
   the work of your hands.
2 Day carries the news to day
   and night brings the message to night.
3 No speech, no word,
   no voice is heard;
4 yet their news goes forth through all the earth,
   their words to the farthest bounds of the world.
   There you pitched a tent for the sun;
5 it comes forth like a bridegroom from his tent,
   like a champion eager to run the race.
6 At the end of the sky is the rising of the sun;
   the boundary of the sky is its course.
   There is nothing hidden from its scorching heat.
7 Your law, Yahweh, is perfect,
   it refreshes the soul.
   Your rule is to be trusted,
   it gives wisdom to the simple.
8 Your precepts, Yahweh, are right,
   they gladden the heart.
   Your command is clear,
   it gives light to the eyes.
9 Fear of you, Yahweh, is holy,
   abiding forever.
   Your decrees are faithful,
   and all of them just.
10 They are more desirable than gold,
   than the purest of gold,
   and sweeter than honey are they,
   than honey oozing from the comb.
11 So in them your servant finds instruction;
   in keeping them is great reward.

12 But who can detect failings?
    From hidden faults forgive me.
13 From presumption restrain your servant,
    and let it not rule me.
    Then I shall be blameless,
    free from grave sin.
14 May the spoken words of my mouth,
    the thoughts of my heart,
    win favor in your sight, O Yahweh,
    my Redeemer, my Rock!

P S A L M   2 0

Prayer for a Leader

1   **M**ay Yahweh answer you in the day of danger;
    may the name of the God of Jacob set you up on high.
2   May God send you help from the sanctuary
    and sustain you from Zion.
3   May God remember all your offerings
    and accept your burnt sacrifices.
4   May God grant you what your heart desires
    and fulfill all your plans.
5   May we shout for joy over your triumph
    and in the name of our God wave our banners;
    may Yahweh fulfill all your petitions.
6   Now I know that God saves the anointed,
    answering from the holy place in heaven
    with saving might.
7   Some boast of chariots and some of horses,
    but we boast in the name of our God.
8   They have bowed down and fallen,
    but we have risen and stand firm.
9   Save us, Yahweh;
    answer when we call.

Thanksgiving for Help in Victory

1 O Yahweh, in your strength I am glad;
   how greatly I rejoice in your victory!
2 You have granted me my heart's desire;
   you refused not the wish of my lips.
3 For you welcomed me with goodly blessings;
   you placed on my head a crown of pure gold.
4 I asked life of you:
   you gave me length of days forever and ever.
5 Great is my glory in your victory;
   majesty and splendor you conferred upon me.
6 For you made me a blessing forever;
   you gladdened me with the joy of your presence.
7 For I trust in you,
   and through your kindness I stand unshaken.
8 May your hand reach all my enemies,
   may your right hand reach my foes!
9 As though in a fiery furnace,
   make them burn when you appear.
   May Yahweh consume them in anger,
   let fire devour them.
10 Destroy their fruit from the earth
   and their posterity from among people.
11 Though they intend evil against you,
   devising plots, they cannot succeed.
12 For you shall put them to flight;
   you shall aim your shafts against them.
13 Be extolled, O Yahweh, in your strength!
   I will sing, chant the praise of your might.

PSALM 22

The Sufferings and Hope of the Virtuous

1 My God, my God, why have you deserted me?
  Far from my prayer, from the words I cry?

2 I call all day, my God, but you never answer;
  all night long I call and cannot rest.

3 Yet, Holy One,
  you who make your home in the praises of Israel—

4 in you our ancestors put their trust;
  they trusted and you rescued them.

5 They called to you for help and were saved;
  they never trusted you in vain.

6 Yet here I am, now more worm than human,
  scorn of all, jest of the people.

7 All who see me jeer at me;
  they toss their heads and sneer:

8 "You relied on Yahweh, let Yahweh save you!
  If Yahweh is your friend, let Yahweh rescue you!"

9 Yet you drew me out of the womb;
  you entrusted me to my mother's breasts.

10 You placed me on your lap from my birth,
  from my mother's womb you have been my God.

11 Do not stand aside: trouble is near
  and I have no one to help me!

12 A herd of bulls surrounds me,
  strong bulls of Bashan close in on me.

13 Their mouths are wide open for me,
  like lions tearing and roaring.

14 I am like water draining away,
  my bones are all disjointed,
  and my heart is like wax
  melting inside me.

15 My throat is drier than baked clay
  and my tongue sticks to my mouth.

16 A pack of dogs surrounds me;
   a gang of villains closes in on me
   They tie me hand and foot
   and leave me lying in the dust of death.
17 I can count every one of my bones;
   they glare and gloat over me.
18 They divide my garments among them
   and cast lots for my clothes.
19 Do not stand aside, Yahweh.
   O my strength, come quickly to my help;
20 rescue my soul from the sword,
   my life from the grip of the dog.
21 Save me from the lion's mouth,
   my poor soul from the wild bulls' horns!
22 Then I shall proclaim your name,
   praise you in full assembly:
23 "You who fear Yahweh, praise God!
   Entire race of Abraham and Sarah, glorify God!
   Entire race of Israel, revere God!
24 For Yahweh has not despised
   or disdained the poor in their poverty,
   has not hidden from them,
   but has answered when they called."
25 You are the theme of my praise in the Great Assembly;
   I perform my vows in the presence of those who fear you.
26 The poor will eat and be satisfied.
   Those who seek you will give praise.
   Long life to their hearts!
27 The whole earth, from end to end,
   will remember and come back to you;
   all the families of the nations will bow down.
28 For you reign, the ruler of nations!
29 Before you all the prosperous of the earth will bow down;
   before you will bow all who go down to the dust.
30 And my soul will live for you;
   my children will serve you.
31 We will proclaim you to generations still to come,
   your righteousness to a people yet unborn.
   All this Yahweh has done.

PSALM 23

Shepherd and Host

1 **Y**ahweh, you are my shepherd;
   I shall not want.
2 In verdant pastures you give me repose.
   Beside restful waters you lead me;
3 you refresh my soul.
   You guide me in right paths
   for your name's sake.
4 Even though I walk in the dark valley
   I fear no evil;
   for you are at my side.
   Your rod and your staff give me courage.
5 You spread the table before me
   in the sight of my foes.
   You anoint my head with oil;
   my cup brims over.
6 Only goodness and kindness follow me
   all the days of my life;
   and I shall dwell in your house
   for years to come.

PSALM 24

An Entrance Song

1 **T**he world and all that is in it belong to Yahweh,
   the earth and all who live on it.
2 Yahweh built it on the deep waters,
   laid its foundations in the oceans' depths.
3 Who has the right to climb Yahweh's mountain?
   Or stand in this holy place?

4 Those who are pure in act and in thought,
who do not worship idols
or make false promises.
5 Yahweh will bless them.
God their Savior will give them salvation.
6 Such are the people who come to God,
who come into the presence of our God.
7 Fling wide the gates,
open the ancient doors,
and the Holy One will come in!
8 Who is this Holy One?
Yahweh, strong and mighty,
Yahweh, victorious in battle!
9 Fling wide the gates,
open the ancient doors,
and the Holy One will come in!
10 Who is this Holy One?
Yahweh, the glorious.

P S A L M   2 5

Prayer in Danger

1 **T**o you, Yahweh, I lift up my soul.
2 O my God, in you I trust.
Let me not be put to shame;
let not my enemies exult over me.
3 Let none that wait for you be put to shame;
let them be ashamed who heedlessly break faith.
4 Make me know your ways, Yahweh;
teach me your paths.
5 Lead me in your truth and teach me,
for you are the God of my salvation;
for you I wait all the day long.

6 Be mindful of your mercy, Yahweh,
and of your steadfast love, for they have been from of old.
7 Remember not the sins of my youth, or my transgressions;
according to your steadfast love remember me,
because of your goodness, Yahweh!
8 Good and upright is Yahweh,
instructing sinners in the way,
9 leading the humble in what is right,
and teaching the poor the way.
10 All the paths of Yahweh are steadfast love and faithfulness
for those who keep God's covenant and decrees.
11 For your name's sake, O Yahweh,
pardon my guilt, for it is great.
12 Who are they who fear you?
Those you instruct in the way that they should choose.
13 They shall abide in prosperity,
and their children shall possess the land.
14 The friendship of Yahweh is with those who fear God,
and God makes known to them the covenant.
15 My eyes are ever toward Yahweh,
who will pluck my feet out of the net.
16 Turn to me, and be gracious to me;
for I am alone and afflicted.
17 Relieve the troubles of my heart,
and bring me out of my suffering.
18 Consider my affliction and my trouble
and forgive all my sins.
19 Take note how my enemies are increasing
and with what violence they hate me.
20 Oh guard my life and deliver me;
let me not be put to shame, for I take refuge in you.
21 May integrity and uprightness preserve me,
for I wait for you.
22 Redeem Israel, O God,
from every danger.

Prayer of an Innocent Person

1   Do me justice, O God,
        for I have walked in integrity,
    and in you I trust without wavering.
2   Search me, O God, and try me;
        test my soul and my heart.
3   For your love is before my eyes,
        and I walk in your truth.
4   I do not stay with deceitful people,
        nor do I consort with hypocrites.
5   I hate the assembly of evildoers,
        and with the wicked I refuse to sit.
6   I wash my hands in innocence,
        and I process around your altar, O God,
7   singing my thanks
        and recounting all your wondrcus deeds.
8   O God, I love the house in which you dwell,
        the resting-place of your glory.
9   Do not gather my soul with those of sinners,
        nor my life with the evil ones.
10 On their hands are crimes,
        and their right hands are full of bribes.
11 But I walk in integrity;
        redeem me and have pity on me.
12 My foot stands on level ground;
        in the assemblies I will bless you, Most High.

Trust in God

1 God, you are my light and my salvation;
whom shall I fear?
You are the stronghold of my life;
of whom shall I be afraid?

2 When evildoers assail me,
uttering slanders against me,
my adversaries and foes,
they shall stumble and fall.

3 Though a host encamp against me,
my heart will not fear;
though war arise against me,
yet I will be confident.

4 One thing have I asked of you, Yahweh,
this I seek:
to dwell in your house
all the days of my life,
to behold your beauty
and to contemplate on your Temple.

5 For you will hide me in your shelter
in the day of trouble,
you will conceal me under the cover of your tent
and will set me high upon a rock.

6 And now my head shall be lifted up
above my enemies on every side.
I will offer in your tent
sacrifices with shouts of joy;
I will sing and make melody to you.

7 Hear me when I cry aloud;
be gracious to me and answer me!

8 You have said, "Seek my face."
My heart says to you, "Your face I do seek."

9   Do not hide your face from me.
    Do not turn your servant away in anger,
    you who have been my help.
    Do not cast me off. Do not forsake me!
    O God of my salvation!
10 Though my father and my mother forsake me,
    you will still accept me.
11 Teach me your way, O God,
    and lead me on a level path
    because of my enemies.
12 Give me not up to the will of my foes,
    for false witnesses have risen against me,
    and they breathe out violence.
13 I believe that I shall see the goodness of Yahweh
    in the land of the living!
14 Wait for Yahweh;
    be strong, and let your heart take courage.
    Yes, wait for God!

P S A L M   2 8

Prayer in Time of Danger

1   **T**o you, Yahweh, I call;
    my Rock, hear me.
    If you do not listen,
    I shall become like those who are dead.
2   Hear the voice of my pleading
    as I cry for help,
    as I lift up my hands in prayer
    to your holy place.
3   Do not drag me away with the wicked,
    with the evildoers
    who speak words of peace to their neighbors
    but have evil in their hearts.

4 Repay them as their actions merit,
for the malice of their deeds.
Repay them for the work of their hands;
give them what they deserve.

5 For they ignore your deeds, Yahweh,
and the work of your hands.

6 Blessed be God,
who has heard my cry, my appeal.

7 You are my strength and my shield.
In you my heart trusts and I find help;
then my heart rejoices,
and I praise you with my song.

8 You are the strength of your people,
the stronghold where your anointed find salvation.

9 Save your people; bless Israel, your heritage.
Be their shepherd and carry them forever.

P S A L M   2 9

God's Majesty in the Storm

1 Give to Yahweh, O heavenly beings,
give to Yahweh glory and strength.

2 Give to Yahweh the glory of God's name;
worship Yahweh in holy array.

3 The voice of Yahweh is upon the waters;
the God of glory thunders upon many waters.

4 The voice of God is powerful;
the voice of Yahweh is full of majesty.

5 The voice of Yahweh breaks the cedars,
breaks the cedars of Lebanon,

6 making Lebanon skip like a calf
and Sirion like a young wild ox.

7 The voice of Yahweh flashes forth flames of fire.

8 The voice of God shakes the wilderness,
   the wilderness of Kadesh.

9 The voice of Yahweh makes the oaks twist
   and strips the forests bare;
   and in God's Temple all cry, "Glory!"

10 Yahweh sits enthroned over the flood;
   God sits enthroned forever.

11 May Yahweh give strength to the people,
   blessing the people with peace!

P S A L M   3 0

A Prayer of Thanksgiving

1 **I** praise you, Yahweh, because you have saved me
   and kept my enemies from gloating over me.

2 I cried to you for help, my God,
   and you healed me.

3 You brought me back from the world of the dead.
   I was with those who go down to the depths below,
   but you restored my life.

4 Sing praise to Yahweh, you faithful people!
   Remember what God has done and give thanks!

5 Yahweh's anger lasts only a moment,
   God's goodness for a lifetime.
   There may be tears during the night,
   but joy comes in the morning.

6 I felt secure and said to myself,
   "I will never be defeated."

7 You are good to me, Yahweh,
   you have kept me safe as in a mountain fortress.
   But when you hid yourself from me,
   I was filled with fear.

8 I called to you, Yahweh;
   I begged for your help.

9 What good will come from my death?
What profit from my going to the grave?
Are dead people able to praise you?
Can they proclaim your unfailing goodness?
10 Hear me, Yahweh, and be merciful!
Help me, Yahweh!
11 You have changed my sadness into a joyful dance;
you have taken off my clothes of mourning
and given me garments of joy.
12 So I will not be silent;
I will sing praise to you.
Yahweh, you are my God;
I will give thanks to you forever.

P S A L M   3 1

Prayer in Time of Ordeal

1 In you, Yahweh, I take refuge;
let me never be disgraced.
In your righteousness deliver me, rescue me;
2 quickly, turn your ear to me!
Be a sheltering rock for me,
and a walled fortress to save me!
3 For you are my rock, my stronghold;
for the sake of your name, guide me and lead me!
4 Pull me out of the net they have spread for me,
for you are my refuge.
5 Into your hands I commit my spirit;
you will redeem me, Yahweh.
6 Faithful God, you hate those
who serve worthless idols,
but I put my trust in you.

7 I will exult and rejoice in your love!
   You, who have seen my wretchedness
   and known the miseries of my soul,
8 have not handed me over to the enemy.
   You have given my feet space to spare.
9 Take pity on me, Yahweh;
   I am in trouble now.
   Sorrow consumes my eyes,
   my throat, my inmost parts.
10 For my life is worn out with sadness,
   my years with sighs;
   my strength collapses under misery,
   and my bones are wasting away.
11 To every one of my oppressors
   I am contemptible;
   loathsome to my neighbors,
   and to my friends a thing of fear.
   Those who see me in the street hurry past me;
12 I am forgotten, as good as dead in their hearts,
   something discarded.
13 They whisper slanders against me,
   threats from every quarter.
   They combine against me,
   Conspiring to take my life.
14 But in you, Yahweh, I trust;
   I say, "You are my God."
15 My fate is in your hand;
   rescue me from the hands of my enemies and persecutors.
16 Let your face smile upon your servant,
   save me in your love.
17 I beg you, Yahweh; do not let me be disgraced,
   let the disgrace fall on the wicked!
   May they go speechless to Sheol,
18 their lying lips struck dumb
   for their insolent slurs on the just,
   for their arrogance and contempt.

19 Yahweh, how great is the goodness
reserved for those who fear you
and bestowed on those who take shelter in you,
for all to see!
20 Safe in your presence you hide them
far from devious human plots;
inside your tent you shelter them
far from the battle of tongues!
21 Blessed be Yahweh,
who shows faithful love for me in a fortress-city!
22 In my terror I exclaimed,
"I have been snatched out of your sight!"
Yet you heard my petition
when I called to you for help.
23 Love Yahweh, all you faithful ones.
Yahweh, protector of the faithful,
will more than repay the arrogant.
24 Be strong, let your heart be bold,
all you who hope in Yahweh!

P S A L M   3 2

Remission of Sin

1 **H**appy are those whose fault is taken away,
whose sin is covered.
2 Happy those whose sin Yahweh does not count,
in whose spirit there is no guile.
3 As long as I would not speak,
my bones wasted away with groaning all day long;
4 for day and night your hand lay heavy upon me.
My strength was dried up as by the summer's heat.

5 Then I acknowledged my sin to you,
  and did not cover my guilt.
  I said, "I confess my faults to you,"
  and you took away the guilt of my sin.
6 For this shall all the faithful pray to you in time of stress.
  Though deep waters rise,
  they shall not reach them.
7 You are my shelter;
  you will protect me from trouble
  and surround me with songs of deliverance.
8 I will instruct you
  and show you the way you should walk;
  I will counsel you and watch over you.
9 Do not be senseless like horses or mules,
  their tempers curbed only by bridle and bit,
  or they will not come near you.
10 Many are the sorrows of the wicked,
  but faithful love surrounds those who trust in you.
11 Rejoice and be glad in Yahweh, you just;
  exult, all you upright of heart.

P S A L M   3 3

Joyful Song to the Creator

1 Sing out your joy to the Creator, good people;
  for praise is fitting for loyal hearts.
2 Give thanks to the Creator upon the harp,
  with a ten-stringed lute sing songs.
3 O sing a new song;
  play skillfully and loudly so all may hear.
4 For the word of the Creator is faithful,
  and all God's works are to be trusted.
5 The Creator loves justice and right
  and fills the earth with faithful love.

6 By the Creator's word the heavens were made,
   by the breath of God's mouth all the stars.
7 The Creator collects the waves of the ocean
   and gathers up the depths of the sea.
8 Let all the earth fear the Creator,
   all who live in the world honor God.
9 The Creator spoke and it came to be;
   commanded, it sprang into existence.
10 The Creator frustrates the plans of the nations,
   overthrows the designs of the peoples.
11 The Creator's own designs shall last forever,
   the plans of God's heart for all ages.
12 They are happy whose God is the Creator,
   the people God has chosen.
13 From the heavens the Creator looks out,
   and sees all the children of the earth.
14 From the heavens God gazes
   on all who dwell on the earth,
15 the Creator who shapes the hearts of them all
   and recollects all their deeds.
16 A ruler is not protected by an army,
   nor a warrior preserved by strength.
17 It is vain to hope for safety in a horse;
   despite its power it cannot save.
18 The Creator looks on those who stand in reverence,
   on those who hope in God's love—
19 to rescue their souls from death,
   to keep them alive in famine.
20 Our soul is waiting for God,
   our help and our shield.
21 In the Creator our hearts find joy.
   We trust in God's holy name.
22 May your faithful love be upon us, O God,
   as we place all our hope in you.

In Praise of God's Justice

1 **I** will bless Yahweh at all times;
praise shall continually be in my mouth.

2 My soul shall rejoice in Yahweh,
let the humble hear it and be glad.

3 Glorify Yahweh with me
and let us exalt God's name together.

4 I sought Yahweh who answered me
and freed me from all my fears.

5 Those who look to Yahweh are radiant,
their faces are never put to shame.

6 The poor called; Yahweh heard
and saved them out of all their troubles.

7 The angel of Yahweh encamps around those
who revere God and rescues them.

8 O taste and see that Yahweh is good!
Blessed are those who trust in God.

9 Revere Yahweh, you saints;
for there is nothing lacking to those who fear God.

10 The lions may grow weak and hungry,
but those who seek Yahweh shall lack nothing good.

11 Come, sons and daughters, listen to me,
I will teach you reverence for Yahweh.

12 Which of you wants to live to the full,
loves long life and enjoys prosperity?

13 Keep your tongue from evil
and your lips from speaking deceit.

14 Turn away from evil and practice good;
seek peace and follow after it.

15 The eyes of Yahweh are toward the just,
and God's ears are open to their cry.

16 The face of Yahweh is against the evildoers,
to root up their memory from the earth.

17 The righteous cried; Yahweh heard
and saved them out of all their troubles.

18 Yahweh is close to the brokenhearted
and rescues those whose spirit is crushed.

19 Many are the afflictions of the just,
but out of them all Yahweh delivers them.

20 Yahweh protects their very bones;
not one of them is broken.

21 Evil shall slay the wicked
and the haters of the just shall be chastised.

22 Yahweh redeems those who serve,
all those taking refuge in God shall go free.

P S A L M   3 5

Prayer for Help against Unjust Enemies

1 O God, accuse my detractors;
attack those who war against me.

2 Flourish shield and buckler!
Stand up in my defense.

3 Brandish lance and battle-ax
before the eyes of my pursuers.
Say to my soul, "I am your salvation."

4 And for those who are out to kill me:
disgrace, dishonor, and ruin.
Drive back, confound, and confuse
those who plot my fall.

5 May they be like chaff before the wind,
with the angel of Yahweh to chase them.

6 Let their path be dark and dangerous,
with the angel of Yahweh to goad them.

7 Without cause they spread a net for me,
a pit they prepare for me.

8 Ruin sneaks up on them unawares.
They are snatched up in the snare that they set,
and they crash into their own trap.

9   Then my soul will celebrate the Most High,
      rejoice that God has saved me.

10 All my bones will declare:
      "Yahweh, who can compare with you
      in rescuing the poor from the strong,
      the oppressed from those who exploit?"

11 Perjurers take the stand,
      charging me with deeds I know nothing about.

12 They repay my charity with evil.
      My soul grieves.

13 Yet, I dressed myself in sackcloth
      when they were sick.
      I afflicted my soul with fasting,
      pouring out prayers in my heart—

14 as if for a friend.
      And, I went about in sorrow and dejection,
      as people do in mourning their mother or father.

15 Gathering together, they are happy now that I have fallen.
      They mock me.
      Complete strangers
      rip me to pieces with shouts,

16 ridiculing me with their taunts,
      grinding their teeth at me.

17 Yahweh, how much longer will you allow this?
      Save my soul from these beasts,
      my only life from these lions.

18 I will give thanks in the Great Assembly,
      glorifying you where the people meet.

19 Do not let my lying enemies gloat over me;
      prevent the sly glances of those who hate me for no reason.

20 They do not discuss peace
      with the peace-loving people of the land.
      Instead they plan deceit.

21 They open their mouths to accuse me.
      "See! See!" they shout.
      "With our own eyes we saw it!"

22 You have seen, Yahweh.
      Do not be silent.
      Do not be far from me!

23 Awake! Defend me!
   Side with me, my God.
24 Yahweh, you are just, so do justice for me.
   Do not let them gloat over me.
25 Stop them from thinking, "Just as we wished!"
   Prevent them from saying, "Now you are down!"
26 To those who celebrate my misfortune,
   shame and disgrace.
   To those who profit at my expense,
   discredit and calamity.
27 But to those who favor my cause,
   let them shout for joy and be glad;
   and may they always sing, "Praise be to our God!"
28 Then my tongue will declare your goodness ·
   and proclaim your praises all day long.

P S A L M   3 6

Human Malice: God's Goodness

1 **S**in speaks to sinners
   in the depths of their hearts.
   No awe of God is before their eyes.
2 They so flatter themselves
   that they do not know their guilt.
3 In their mouths are lies and foolishness.
   Gone is all wisdom.
4 They plot the downfall of goodness
   as they lie on their beds.
   They set their feet on evil ways,
   they hold to what is evil.
5 Your love, Yahweh, reaches to heaven;
   your faithfulness to the skies.
6 Your justice is like a mountain—
   your judgments like the deep.
   To all creation you give protection.

7 Your people find refuge
   in the shelter of your wings.
8 They feast on the riches of your house;
   they drink from the stream of your delight.
9 You are the source of life,
   and in your light we see light.
10 Continue your love to those who know you,
   doing justice to the upright in heart.
11 Let the foot of the proud not crush me,
   nor the hand of the wicked drive me away.
12 See how the evildoers have fallen!
   Flung down, they shall never rise.

P S A L M   3 7

The Reward of the Just

1 **F**ret not because of the wicked;
   be not envious of wrongdoers!
2 For they will soon fade like the grass
   and wither like the green herb.
3 Trust in Yahweh and do good
   so you will dwell in the land and enjoy security.
4 Take delight in Yahweh,
   who will give you the desires of your heart.
5 Commit your way to Yahweh;
   trust in God who will act,
6 bringing forth your vindication as the light,
   and your right as the noonday sun.
7 Be still before Yahweh, and wait patiently;
   fret not over those who prosper,
   over those who carry out evil.
8 Refrain from anger and forsake wrath!
   Fret not; it tends only to evil.
9 For the wicked shall be cut off,
   but those who wait for Yahweh shall possess the land.

10 Yet a little while and the wicked will be no more;
though you look well at their place,
they will not be there.
11 But the meek shall possess the land
and delight themselves in abundance.
12 The wicked plot against the righteous
and gnash their teeth at them;
13 but Yahweh laughs at the wicked,
for God sees that their day is coming.
14 The wicked draw their swords and bend their bows
to bring down the poor and the needy,
to slay those whose ways are upright.
15 Their swords shall enter their own hearts,
and their bows shall all be broken.
16 Better is the little that the just have
than the abundance of the wicked;
17 for the arms of the wicked shall be broken,
but Yahweh upholds the just.
18 Yahweh knows the days of the blameless,
and their heritage will abide for ever.
19 They are not put to shame in evil times;
in the days of famine they have abundance.
20 But the wicked perish;
the enemies of Yahweh are like the beauty of the pastures:
they vanish—like smoke they vanish.
21 The wicked borrow and cannot pay back,
but the just are generous and give;
22 for those blessed by Yahweh shall possess the land,
but those cursed shall be cut off.
23 A person's steps are confirmed by Yahweh;
God delights in the way of the virtuous.
24 Though falling, they shall not be cast headlong,
for the hand of Yahweh supports them.
25 I have been young and now I am old;
yet I have not seen the just forsaken
or their children begging for bread.
26 They are ever giving liberally and lending,
and their children become a blessing.

27 Depart from evil and do good;
   so you shall abide forever.
28 For Yahweh loves justice
   and will not forsake the saints.
   The righteous shall be preserved forever.
   but the children of the wicked shall be cut off.
29 The righteous shall possess the land
   and dwell upon it forever.
30 The mouths of the just utter wisdom,
   and their tongues speak justice.
31 The law of God is in their hearts;
   their steps do not slip.
32 The wicked watch the just
   and seek to slay them.
33 Yahweh will not abandon them to their power
   or let them be condemned when they are brought to trial.
34 Wait for Yahweh and keep God's way.
   Yahweh will promote you to possess the land;
   you will look on the destruction of the wicked.
35 I have seen the wicked, overbearing
   and towering like a cedar of Lebanon.
36 Again I passed by, and behold, they were no more;
   though I sought them, they could not be found.
37 Mark the blameless and behold the upright,
   for there is a future for those of peace.
38 But sinners shall all be destroyed;
   the future of the wicked shall be cut off.
39 The salvation of the just is from Yahweh,
   their refuge in time of trouble.
40 Yahweh helps them and delivers them—
   delivers them from the wicked and saves them—
   because they take refuge in God.

Prayer of the Afflicted

1 O God, rebuke me not in your anger,
  nor chastise me in your wrath!
2 For your arrows have sunk into me,
  and your hand has come down on me.
3 There is no wholeness in my flesh
  because of your indignation.
  There is no health in my bones
  because of my sin,
4 for my iniquities have overwhelmed me.
  They weigh like a burden too heavy for me.
5 My wounds grow foul and fester
  because of my foolishness.
6 I am utterly bowed down and prostrate:
  all day I go about mourning.
7 My loins are filled with burning pain,
  and there is no wholeness in my flesh.
8 I am utterly spent and crushed;
  I groan because of the anguish of my heart.
9 Yahweh, all my longing is known to you;
  my sighing is not hidden from you.
10 My heart throbs and my strength fails me;
   the light of my eyes has gone from me.
11 My friends and companions stand aloof from my plague,
   and my neighbors stand afar off.
12 Those who seek my life lay their snares;
   those who seek my hurt speak of ruin
   and meditate treachery all the day long.
13 But I am like the deaf—I do not hear;
   like the dumb who do not open their mouths.
14 Yes, I am like those who do not hear
   and in whose mouths are no rebukes.
15 But for you, Yahweh, I wait;
   it is you, my God, who will answer.
16 For I pray, "Only let them not rejoice over me,
   who boast against me when my foot slips!"

17 For I am ready to fall,
and my pain is ever with me.
18 I confess my iniquity;
I am sorry for my sin.
19 Those who are my foes without cause are strong,
and many are those who hate me wrongfully.
20 Those who render me evil for good are my adversaries
because I follow after good.
21 Do not forsake me;
O my God, be not far from me!
22 Make haste to help me,
my salvation!

P S A L M   3 9

No Abiding City

1 I said: "I will be watchful of my ways
for fear that I should sin with my tongue.
I will put a curb on my lips
when the wicked stand before me."
2 I was dumb, silent and refrained from speech.
But my grief was stirred up.
3 My heart was burning within me.
At the thought of it, the fire blazed up
and my tongue burst into speech:
4 "Yahweh, you have shown me my end.
How short is the length of my days!
Now I know how fleeting my life is.
5 You have given me a short span of days;
my life is as nothing in your sight.
A mere breath is human life,
6 a mere shadow passing by;
a mere breath, the riches they hoard,
not knowing who will have them."

7 And now, Yahweh, is there anything to wait for?
All my hope is in you.

8 Free me from all my sins,
do not make me the foil of the fool.

9 I was silent, shutting my lips,
for this was all your doing.

10 Take away your whip from me;
I am beaten by the blows of your hand.

11 You punish the sins of the people and correct them:
like the moth you devour all they treasure.
Mortals are no more than a breath.

12 Yahweh, hear my prayer.
Listen to my weeping.
I am a wanderer before you,
a pilgrim like my ancestors:

13 turn your gaze from me so that I may take a breath,
before I leave, and cease to be!

P S A L M   4 0

Song of Praise and Prayer for Help

1 I waited and waited for you, Yahweh!
Now at last you have turned to me
and heard my cry for help.

2 You have lifted me out of the horrible pit,
out of the slough of the marsh;
you set my feet on a rock
and steadied my steps.

3 Yahweh, you have put a new song in my mouth—
a song of praise.
Many will look on in awe
and will put their trust in you.

4 Happy those who put their trust in Yahweh
and do not side with rebels who stray after false gods.

5 How many wonders you have done for us,
Yahweh, our God!
How many plans you have made for us!
You have no equal.
I want to proclaim your deeds again and again,
but they are more than I can count.

6 You, who wanted no sacrifice or oblation,
opened my ear;
you asked no holocaust or sacrifice for sin.

7 Then I said, "Here I am! I have come!"

8 In the scroll of the book it is prescribed for me
to obey your will.
My God, I have always loved your Law
from the depths of my being.

9 I have always proclaimed the justice of Yahweh
in the Great Assembly;
nor do I mean to stop proclaiming,
as you know well.

10 I have never kept your justice hidden within myself,
but have spoken of your faithfulness and saving help;
I have made no secret of your love and faithfulness
in the Great Assembly.

11 For your part, Yahweh,
do not withhold your mercy from me!
May your love and faithfulness constantly protect me.

12 More misfortunes beset me than I can count.
My sins close in on me until I cannot see;
they outnumber the hair on my head.
My courage is running out.

13 Oh come and rescue me, Yahweh,
come quickly and help me!

14 May those who seek to kill and destroy me
suffer shame and confusion!
Calamity and disgrace on those who enjoy my ruin!

15 May they be dismayed with shame,
those who say to me, "Aha! Aha!"

16 But joy and gladness
   for all who seek you!
   To all who love your saving power
   give constant cause to say, "God be glorified."
17 To me, afflicted and poor,
   come quickly.
   My Helper, my Savior, my God,
   come and do not delay!

P S A L M   4 1

The Prayer of One Who Is Sick

1 **H**appy those who aid the poor and the lowly.
   God will help them when they are in trouble.
2 Yahweh will protect and preserve them,
   will make them happy in the land,
   and will not abandon them to the power of their enemies.
3 Yahweh will help them when they are sick
   and restore them to health.
4 I said, "I have sinned against you, God;
   be merciful to me and cure me!"
5 My enemies speak evil about me.
   They say, "When will you die and be forgotten?"
6 Those who come to see me are not sincere;
   they gather all the bad news about me
   and then go out and spread it everywhere.
7 All who hate me whisper together about me;
   they imagine the worst about me.
8 They say, "You are fatally ill
   and will never leave your bed again."

9 Even my best friend—the one I trusted most,
the one who shared my food—
has turned against me.

10 Be merciful to me, Yahweh,
and restore my health.

11 I will know that you love me
because they will not triumph over me.

12 You will help me because I do what is right;
you will keep me in your presence forever.

13 Let us praise Yahweh,
praise the God of Israel now and forever!
Amen! Amen!

P S A L M   4 2

The Exile's Longing for God's Temple

1 Like the deer that yearns
for running streams,
so my soul is yearning
for you, my God.

2 My soul is thirsting for God, the living God.
When can I enter to see the face of God?

3 My tears have become my food night and day,
and I hear it said all day long:
"Where is your God?"

4 I will remember all these things
as I pour out my soul:
how I would lead the joyous procession
into the house of God,
with cries of gladness and thanksgiving,
the multitude wildly happy.

5 Why are you so sad, my soul?
Why sigh within me?
Hope in God;
for I will yet praise my savior and my God.

6 My soul is downcast within me
   when I think of you,
   from the land of Jordan and Mount Hermon,
   from the Hill of Mizar.
7 Deep is calling on deep
   as the waterfalls roar:
   your breakers and all your waves
   crashed over me.
8 By day Yahweh will send loving·kindness;
   by night I will sing praise to the God of my life.
9 I will say to God, my rock:
   "Why have you forgotten me?
   Why do I go mourning,
   oppressed by the foe?"
10 With cries that pierce me to the heart,
   my enemies revile me,
   saying to me all day:
   "Where is your God?"
11 Why are you oppressed, my soul—
   why cry within me?
   Hope in God; I will praise Yahweh,
   my savior and my God.

P S A L M   4 3

Lament

1 Do me justice, O God, and plead my cause
   against a faithless people;
   from the deceitful and unjust, rescue me.
2 For you, O God, are my stronghold.
   Why do you keep me so far away?
   Why must I go about in mourning,
   oppressed by the enemy?
3 Send forth your light and your truth—
   they shall guide me;
   let them bring me to your holy mountain,
   to your dwelling place.

4 Then will I go in to the altar of God,
   the God of my delight and joy;
   then will I praise you with the harp,
   O God, my God!
5 Why are you so downcast, O my soul?
   Why do you sigh within me?
   Put your hope in God, for I shall again be thankful
   in the presence of my savior and my God.

P S A L M   4 4

Lament

1 O God, we have heard with our ears,
     our ancestors have told us
   all the deeds that you did in their days,
   all the work of your hand in days long ago.
2 You planted them in the land and drove the nations out;
   you made them strike root, scattering the other peoples.
3 It was not our ancestors' swords that won them the land,
   nor their arm that gave them the victory—
   but your right hand and your arm
   and the light of your face.
   Such was your favor to them.
4 You are my God;
   at your bidding Jacob is victorious.
5 By your help we will push back our enemies;
   in your name we will trample our adversaries.
6 I will not trust in my bow;
   my sword will not win me the victory,
7 for you deliver us from our foes
   and put all our enemies to shame.

8 In you, God, have we gloried all day long,
   and we will praise your name forever.

9 But now you have rejected and humbled us
   and no longer lead our armies into battle.

10 You have made us retreat before the enemy,
   and our foes plunder us as they will.

11 You have given us up to be slaughtered like sheep
   and scattered us among the nations.

12 You have sold your people for next to nothing
   and had no profit from the sale.

13 You have exposed us to the taunts of our neighbors,
   to the scorn and contempt of all around.

14 You have made us a byword among the nations,
   a laughingstock to the people,

15 so my disgrace confronts me all day long,
   and I am covered with shame

16 at the shouts of those who reproach and abuse me
   as the enemy takes revenge.

17 All this has happened to us, but we do not forget you
   and have not betrayed your covenant;

18 we have not gone back on our purpose,
   nor have our feet strayed from your path.

19 Yet you crushed us as the sea serpent was crushed
   and covered us with darkness.

20 If we had forgotten the name of our God
   and spread our hands in prayer to any other,

21 would not God find this out—
   for God knows the secrets of the heart.

22 Because of you we face death all day long
   and are considered as sheep for slaughter.

23 Rouse yourself—why do you sleep?
   Awake, do not reject us forever.

24 Why do you hide your face,
   forgetting our misery and our sufferings?

25 For we sink down to the dust
   and cling to the ground.

26 Rise up and come to our help;
   because of your unfailing love, set us free.

Royal Wedding Song

1 My heart overflows with a goodly theme;
  I address my verses to the king;
  my tongue is like the pen of a ready scribe.

2 You are the fairest of all;
  grace is poured upon your lips;
  thus God has blessed you forever.

3 Gird your sword upon your side, O mighty one,
  clothe yourself with glory and majesty!

4 In your splendor ride forth victoriously
  for the cause of justice and to defend the truth;
  let your right hand show your wondrous deeds!

5 Your arrows are sharp
  and pierce the hearts of your enemies.

6 Your throne endures forever and ever.
  Your royal scepter is a scepter of equity.

7 You love justice and hate wickedness,
  therefore God, your God, has anointed you
  with the oil of gladness;

8 your robes are all fragrant with myrrh and aloes and cassia.
  From ivory palaces, stringed instruments bring you joy;

9 daughters of kings come to meet you;
  at your right hand stands the queen in gold of Ophir.

10 Hear, O daughter, consider, and turn your ear;
   forget your people and your ancestor's home.

11 The king will desire your beauty.

12 The people of Tyre are here with gifts,
   the richest of the people seeking your favor.

13 The princess is decked in her chamber
   with gold-woven robes;

14 in many-colored robes she enters with her virgin companions,
   her escort in her train.

15 With joy and gladness they are led along
   as they enter the palace of the king.
16 The place of your ancestors your children shall have;
   you will make them rulers through all the earth.
17 I will cause your name to be celebrated in all generations;
   therefore the peoples will praise you forever and ever.

PSALM 46

God, the Refuge of Israel

1 God is our refuge and our strength,
   our ever-present help in distress.
2 Though the earth trembles,
   and mountains slide into the sea,
   we have no fear.
3 Waters foam and roar,
   and mountains shake at their surging;
   but the God of hosts is with us—
   our stronghold, the God of Israel.
4 There is a river
   whose streams give joy to the city of God,
   the holy dwelling of the Most High.
5 God is in its midst; it stands firm.
   God will aid it at the break of day.
6 Even if nations are in chaos, and kingdoms fall,
   God's voice resounds; the earth melts away.
7 Yahweh is with us;
   the God of Israel is our stronghold.
8 Come! See the deeds of the Most High,
   the marvelous things God has done on earth;
9 all over the world, God has stopped wars—
   breaking bows, splintering spears,
   burning the shields with fire.

10 "Be still! and know that I am God,
    exalted among the nations, exalted upon the earth."
11 The Most High is with us;
    our stronghold is the God of Israel.

P S A L M   4 7

Yahweh, Ruler of Israel

1   All you peoples, clap your hands;
    raise a joyful shout to God.
2   For the Most High is awesome,
    glorious over all the earth.
3   God subdues peoples under us
    and puts nations at our feet.
4   The God of Love chooses for us our inheritance,
    the pride of Jacob.
5   God has ascended amid shouts of joy and trumpet peals.
6   Sing praise to God, sing praise,
7   for God is the Most High over all the earth.
    Sing hymns of praise.
8   God rules over all the nations;
    God sits upon the holy throne.
9   The nobles of the nations are gathered
    with the people of the God of Abraham and Sarah.
    For the guardians of the earth are God's.
    Over all is God exalted.

Thanksgiving for Jerusalem's Deliverance

1 **G**reat is Yahweh and worthy of praise
   in the city of our God,
   whose holy mountain, fairest of heights,
2 is the joy of all the earth.
   Mount Zion, far up in the north,
   is the city of the Most High.
3 God is in its castles,
   renowned as a stronghold.
4 The rulers assemble;
   they advance together.
5 They also see, and at once are amazed,
   terrified, and put to flight.
6 Trembling seizes them there;
   anguish, like a woman's in labor,
7 as though a wind from the east
   were shattering ships of Tarshish.
8 As we had heard, so now we see
   in the city of the God of hosts,
   in the city of our God.
   God makes it secure forever.
9 O God, we ponder your faithful love
   within your Temple.
10 Like your name, O God,
   so your praise reaches the ends of the earth.
   Your right hand is full of justice.
11 Let Mount Zion rejoice,
   let the villages of Judah be glad
   because of your judgments.
12 Walk about Zion, go all around it.
   Count the towers.
13 Study the ramparts well;
   examine the castles,
   that you may tell the next generation
14 that such is God.
   Forever and ever our God will guide us.

The Foolishness of Trusting in Riches

1   **H**ear this!
    Listen, all people everywhere,
2   both great and small alike,
    rich and poor together.
3   My heart is full of insight;
    I will speak words of wisdom.
4   I will turn my attention to a proverb
    and unravel its meaning as I play the harp.
5   I am not afraid in times of danger,
    when I am surrounded by wicked enemies—
6   those who trust in their riches
    and boast of their great wealth.
7   People can never redeem themselves,
    cannot pay God the price for their ransom,
8   because the payment for their life is too great.
    What they can pay will never be enough
9   to keep them from destruction,
    to let them live forever.
10 They see that even the wise die,
    as well as the foolish and senseless.
    They all leave their riches to others.
11 Their tombs are their homes forever;
    there they stay for all time,
    even though they once had lands of their own.
12 Their greatness cannot keep them from death;
    they will die like the animals.
13 See what happens to those who trust in themselves—
    the fate of those who are satisfied with their wealth:
14 they are doomed to die like sheep,
    and death is their shepherd.
    The righteous will rule over them in the morning
    as their bodies decay in the land of the dead,
    far from their homes!

15 But God will redeem me
    and will take me from the power of death.
16 Don't be afraid when people become rich,
    when their wealth grows even greater.
17 They cannot take it with them when they die;
    their wealth will not go down to the grave with them.
18 Even if they are satisfied with this life
    and are praised because they are successful,
19 they will join all their ancestors in death,
    where the darkness lasts forever.
20 Riches cannot keep them from death;
    they will die like the beasts of the field.

P S A L M   5 0

The Acceptable Sacrifice

1 The Mighty One, God our Redeemer,
   speaks and summons the earth
   from the rising of the sun to its setting.
2 From Zion, the perfection of beauty,
   God shines forth.
3 Our God comes and does not keep silence.
   Before God is a devouring fire;
   round about God a raging storm.
4 God calls the heavens above
   and the earth to the people's trial:
5 "Gather to me my faithful ones,
   who made a covenant with me by sacrifice!"
6 The heavens proclaim God's justice,
   for God is judge!
7 "Listen, my people, I will speak;
   Israel, I will testify against you.
   I am God, your God.

8   I do not rebuke you for your sacrifices;
     your burnt offerings are continually before me.

9   I will accept no bull from your house,
     nor goat from your folds;

10   for every animal of the forest is mine,
      the cattle on a thousand hills.

11   I know all the birds of the air,
      and all that moves in the field is mine.

12   If I were hungry, I would not tell you;
      for the world and all that is in it is mine.

13   Do I eat the flesh of strong bulls
      or drink the blood of goats?

14   Offer to God a sacrifice of praise
      and fulfill your vows to the Most High.

15   Call upon me in the day of trouble;
      I will deliver you, and you shall honor me.''

16   But to the wicked God says:
      ''What right have you to recite my laws
      or take my covenant on your lips?

17   For you hate discipline,
      and you cast my words behind you.

18   When you see a thief, you become friends;
      and you keep company with adulterers.

19   You give your mouth free rein for evil,
      and your tongue frames deceit.

20   You sit and speak against others;
      you slander your own family.

21   These things you have done and I have been silent.
      You thought that I was one like yourself.
      But now I rebuke you and lay the charge before you.

22   Consider this, then, you who forget God,
      or I will seize you so none can save you!

23   Those who bring praise as their sacrifice honor me.
      To those who order their way aright—
      I will show the salvation of God!''

Miserere

1   In your goodness, O God, have mercy on me;
    with gentleness wipe away my faults.
2   Cleanse me of guilt;
    free me from my sins.
3   My faults are always before me;
    my sins haunt my mind.
4   I have sinned against you and no other—
    knowing that my actions were wrong in your eyes.
    Your judgment is what I deserve;
    your sentence supremely fair.
5   As you know I was born in guilt,
    from conception a sinner at heart.
6   But you love true sincerity,
    so you teach me the depths of wisdom.
7   Until I am clean, bathe me with hyssop;
    wash me until I am whiter than snow.
8   Infuse me with joy and gladness;
    let these bones you have crushed dance for joy.
9   Please do not stare at my sins;
    blot out all my guilt.
10 Create a pure heart in me, O my God;
    renew me with a steadfast spirit.
11 Don't drive me away from your presence,
    or take your Holy Spirit from me.
12 Once more be my savior; revive my joy.
    Strengthen and sharpen my still weak spirit.
13 And I will teach transgressors your ways;
    then sinners will return to you, too.
14 Release me from death, God my Savior,
    and I will announce your justice.
15 Open my lips,
    and my tongue will proclaim your glory.
16 Sacrifices give you no pleasure;
    if I offered a holocaust, you would refuse it.

17 My sacrifice is this broken spirit.
You will not disdain a contrite and humbled heart.
18 Graciously show your favor to Zion;
rebuild the walls of Jerusalem.
19 Then there will be sacrifice to please you—
oblations and burnt offerings—
and young bulls to be offered on your altar.

P S A L M   5 2

The Fate of Cynics

1 **W**hy boast of your wickedness, you tyrant,
plotting wild lies all day against God's loyal servant?
2 Your slanderous tongue is razor sharp.
3 You love evil rather than good—
falsehood, not speaking the truth.
4 You love cruel gossip and slanderous talk.
5 So God will bring you down to the ground,
sweep you away, leave you ruined and homeless—
uprooted from the land of the living.
6 The just will look on, awestruck,
and laugh at your plight.
7 "This is the one," they say,
"who does not make God a refuge,
but trusts in great wealth
and takes refuge in harmful plots."
8 But I am like a spreading olive tree in God's house,
for I trust in God's unfailing love forever and ever.
9 I will praise you forever for what you have done
and glorify your name in the presence of those who love you.

Lament over Corruption

1 **T**he fools say in their hearts,
   "There is no God."
   They are corrupt, and their ways are evil.
   There are none who do good.
2 God looks down from heaven
   to see if there are any that are wise,
   any who seek after God.
3 Everyone has fallen away;
   they are all alike—corrupt.
   There are none that do good—no, not even one.
4 Have those evildoers no understanding—
   those who eat up my people as they eat bread
   and do not call upon God?
5 There they are, overwhelmed with fear,
   in fear whose source is unknown!
   For God will scatter the bones of evildoers;
   they will be put to shame, for God has rejected them.
6 Oh, that deliverance for Israel would come from Zion!
   When God restores the well-being of faithful people,
   then Jacob will rejoice and Israel be glad.

Confident Prayer

1 **S**ave me, O God, by the power of your name,
   and defend me by your might.
2 O God, hear my prayer;
   listen to my supplication.
3 The insolent rise to attack me;
   the ruthless seek my life;
   they have no regard for God.

4 But God is my helper,
   the one who sustains my life.
5 May their own evil recoil on those who slander me!
   Silence them by your truth, O God.
6 I will offer you a willing sacrifice
   and praise your name, for it is good.
7 God has rescued me from every trouble,
   and I have seen the defeat of my enemies.

P S A L M   5 5

Prayer in Persecution

1 Hear my prayer, O God;
   do not hide yourself from my petition.
2 Listen to me and answer me.
   In restlessness I groan and am troubled
3 because of the voice of the enemy,
   because of the threats of the wicked.
   For they engulf me with their mischief,
   and in anger they assault me.
4 My heart is distressed within me,
   and terrors of death come down on me.
5 Fear and trembling get hold of me,
   and horror overwhelms me.
6 So I said, "Oh, had I the wings of a dove!
   Then I would fly away and be at rest.
7 Yes, then I would flee far away
   and lodge in the desert.
8 I would hasten to my place of refuge,
   from this raging wind and storm."
9 Destroy them, my Refuge, confuse their speech,
   for I have seen violence and strife in the city.
10 Day and night they go about on the walls;
   evil and trouble are in its center.

11 Violence is within the city,
and from the market place oppression
and fraud are never absent.

12 For it is not an enemy who reproaches me;
that I could bear.
It is not a rival who taunts me,

13 but you, my other self,
my companion and my close friend!

14 We who together enjoyed comradeship,
at whose side I walked
in the festive throng to the house of God.

15 Let destruction seize them;
let them go down alive to Sheol;
for evil is in their dwelling, it is in their heart.

16 But as for me, I will call on God,
who will save me.

17 Evening, morning, and noon,
I will grieve and sigh;
and my Liberator will hear my voice.

18 God will rescue my soul
from those who war against me;
for they who oppose me are many.

19 God—the One who sits enthroned from of old—
will hear me and humble them,
because in them there has been no change
and they do not fear God.

20 Each one lays hands on allies
and violates their pact.

21 Their mouths are smoother than butter,
but in their hearts there is war;
their words are softer than oil,
yet they are drawn swords.

22 Cast your cares on God, who will sustain you
and will never allow the righteous to fall.
23 But you, O God, will bring down the wicked
into the pit of destruction;
the deceitful shall not live out half their days.
I will trust in you.

P S A L M   5 6

Reliance on God

1 Be gracious to me, O God, for the enemy persecutes me;
my adversaries harass me all day long.
2 All day long my watchful foes persecute me;
countless are those who oppress me.
3 Appear on high in my day of fear.
I put my trust in you.
4 With God to help me I will stand firm.
In God I trust, and I shall not be afraid.
What can mortals do to me?
5 All day long they plot to harm me:
all their thoughts are hostile.
6 They are on the lookout;
they conspire and spy on my footsteps.
But while they lie in wait for me,
it is they who will not escape.
7 O God, in your anger bring ruin on the nations.
8 Enter my lament in your book;
store every tear in your flask.
9 Then my enemies will be turned back
on the day when I call upon you;
10 for this I know—that God is with me.

11 In God I trust and shall not be afraid.
    What can mortals do to me?
12 I have bound myself with vows to you, O God,
    and will fulfill them with thank offerings;
13 for you have rescued me from death—
    to walk in your presence, in the light of life.

PSALM 5 7

Prayer for Deliverance

1   **H**ave mercy on me, God, have mercy.
    In you my soul takes shelter;
    I take shelter in the shadow of your wings
    until the danger passes.
2   I call out to God the Most High,
    to God who has blessed me:
3   to send from heaven and save me,
    to rebuke those who trample me.
    May God send me faithfulness and love.
4   I lie down among the lions
    hungry for human prey;
    their teeth are spears and arrows,
    their tongue like a sharp sword.
5   Be exalted above the heavens, God.
    Let your glory shine on the earth!
6   They set a snare where I was walking
    when I was bowed with care;
    they dug a pit for me,
    but fell into it themselves!
7   My heart is steadfast, God,
    my heart is steadfast;
    I mean to sing and play for you.

8 Awake, my soul
   awake, lyre and harp,
   I mean to wake the dawn!
9 I mean to thank you among the peoples,
   to sing your praise among the nations.
10 Your love reaches to the heavens,
   your faithfulness to the clouds.
11 Rise high above the heavens, God,
   let your glory cover the earth!

P S A L M   5 8

A Prayer for God to Punish the Wicked

1 Do you really give a just decision, you rulers?
   Do you judge all persons fairly?
2 No! You think only of the evil you will do
   and commit crimes of violence in the land.
3 Evildoers go astray all their lives;
   they tell lies from the day they are born.
4 They are full of poison, like snakes;
   they stop up their ears, like a deaf cobra,
5 which does not hear the voice of the snake charmer
   or the chant of the clever magician.
6 Smash their teeth, O God;
   tear out the fangs of these fierce lions!
7 May they disappear like water draining away;
   may they be crushed like weeds on the path.
8 May they be like snails that dissolve into slime;
   may they be like a baby born dead
   that never sees the light.

9   Before they know it, they are cut down like a thornbush;
in fierce anger God will blow them away
while they are still living.

10   The just will be glad when they see sinners punished;
they will wade through the blood of the wicked.

11   People will say, "The just are indeed rewarded;
there is a God who judges the world!"

P S A L M   5 9

Appeal to God, the Stronghold

1   **S**ave me, O God, from my enemies;
protect me from those who attack me.

2   Save me from the evildoers
and deliver me from those who lust for blood.

3   Notice, they conceal themselves in ambush;
for no offense or fault of mine,

4   for no guilt of mine, they prepare to attack.
Awake, see and help me!

5   Yahweh, God of Israel,
stir yourself and chasten the nations;
have no mercy on these villainous traitors.

6   At night they slink back like wild dogs,
roaming the town and howling.

7   Their tongues drip blasphemy,
and their mouths are filled with insults.
"After all," they snap, "who will hear us?"

8   But you, O God, will laugh at them.
You make light of all the nations.

9   I turn to you, O God my Strength,
for you are my stronghold.

10   Gracious God!
Come to my aid
so that I can stare triumphantly on my foes.

11 Slay them, or my people might be seduced;
    harry them by your power and knock them down.
    You are our shield.
12 For the sins of their mouths,
    for the blasphemies and lies that they speak,
    let them be strangled in their pride.
13 Destroy them in your anger—
    annihilate them from our midst.
    Show them that you are the ruler—
    over Jacob and all of the earth.
14 At nightfall they come back like curs,
    roaming the town and howling.
15 They wander in search of food,
    snarling till they have their fill.
16 As for me, I will sing of your power
    and every morning acclaim your faithful love,
    because you have been my stronghold,
    a shelter in the time of my trouble.
17 My Strength, I always turn to you,
    for you, God, are my fortress,
    the God who loves me.

PSALM 60

Prayer after Defeat

1 O God, you have rejected us and broken our defenses;
    you have been angry. Now restore us.
2 You have rocked the country and torn it open.
    Repair the cracks in it, for it is tottering.
3 You have made your people feel hardships;
    you have given us wine that makes us stagger.
4 But you have raised for those who fear you
    a banner to which they may flee out of bowshot,

5 that your loved ones may escape.
Help us by your right hand and answer us!

6 God promised in the sanctuary:
"In triumph I will apportion Shechem,
and measure off the valley of Succoth. ⸭

7 Mine is Gilead, and mine Manasseh;
Ephraim is the helmet for my head;
Judah, my scepter.

8 Moab shall serve as my washbowl;
upon Edom I will set my sandal.
I will triumph over Philistia."

9 Who will bring me into the fortified city?
Who will lead me into Edom?

10 Have not you, O God, rejected us,
so that you do not march forth with our armies?

11 Give us aid against the foe,
for worthless is all other help.

12 With you we shall do valiantly;
it is you, God, who will tread down our foes.

PSALM 61

Prayer of an Exile

1 Hear my cry, O God; listen to my prayer.
2 From the end of the earth
I call to you with fainting heart.
Lift me up and set me high upon a rock.

3 For you have been my shelter,
a tower of strength against the enemy.

4 In your tent will I make my home forever
and find my refuge under the shelter of your wings.

5 For you, O God, have accepted my vows
and granted me the heritage of all who honor your name.

6 To the leader's life add length of days,
  year upon year for many generations.
7 The ruler may dwell in God's presence forever,
  preserved by true and faithful love.
8 So will I ever sing psalms in praise of your name
  as I fulfil my vows day after day.

PSALM 62

God, the Rock of Strength

1 For God alone my soul waits.
  My help comes from God,
2 who alone is my rock, my stronghold, my fortress:
  I stand firm.
3 How long will you all attack me
  to break me down
  as though I were a tottering wall
  or a sagging fence?
4 Their plan is only to destroy.
  They take pleasure in lies.
  With their mouths they utter blessing,
  but in their hearts they curse.
5 For God alone my soul waits;
  for my hope comes from God,
6 who alone is my rock, my stronghold, my fortress.
  I stand firm.
7 In God is my salvation and glory,
  the rock of my strength.
8 All you people, take refuge in God.
  Trusting at all times,
  pour out your hearts before God, our Refuge.

9   Common folk are only a breath;
    those of rank, an illusion.
    Placed in the scales, they rise;
    they weigh less than a breath.
10 Do not put your trust in oppression
    nor in vain hopes or plunder.
    Do not set your heart on riches
    even when they abound.
11 For God has declared only one thing;
    only two do I know:
    that to you alone belongs power,
12 and that you, Yahweh, are steadfast love.
    Surely you repay all
    according to their deeds.

P S A L M   6 3

Ardent Longing for God

1   **O** God, you are my God whom I eagerly seek;
    for you my flesh longs and my soul thirsts
    like the earth, parched, lifeless, and without water.
2   I have gazed toward you in the sanctuary
    to see your power and your glory.
3   For your love is better than life;
    my lips shall glorify you.
4   Thus will I praise you while I live;
    lifting up my hands, I will call upon your name.
5   As with the riches of a banquet shall my soul be filled,
    and with exultant lips my mouth shall praise you.
6   On my bed I will remember you,
    and through the night watches I will meditate on you:
7   because you are my help,
    and in the shadow of your wings I shout for joy.
8   My soul clings to you;
    your right hand upholds me.

9 But they shall be destroyed who seek my life;
   they shall go down to the depths of the earth.
10 They shall be delivered over to the sword
   and shall be the food of jackals.
11 However, I shall rejoice in God.
   Everyone who swears by God shall give praise,
   but the mouths of those who speak falsely shall be silenced.

P S A L M   6 4

The Punishment for Slanderers

1 **H**ear me, O God, hear my lament.
   Protect me from the threats of the enemy.
2 Hide me from the conspiracy of the wicked,
   from the turbulent mob of evildoers
3 who sharpen their tongues like swords
   and aim their cruel words like arrows.
4 In ambush they shoot down the innocent,
   shooting suddenly, themselves unseen.
5 They arrogantly hide their snares,
   sure that none will see them.
6 They plot injustice with skill and cunning,
   with evil purpose and deep design.
7 But God shoots them down with arrows.
   Their overthrow is sudden.
8 They may repeat their wicked tales,
   but their mischievous tongues are their undoing.
   All who see their fate shake their heads;
   all are afraid.
9 "This is God's work," they proclaim;
   they learn their lesson from what God has done.
10 The righteous rejoice and seek refuge in God,
   and all the upright praise God.

Thanksgiving for God's Blessings

1 Our hymn of praise belongs to you,
O God, in Zion.
To you must vows be fulfilled,
you who answer our prayers.

2 All flesh must come to you
with the burden of its sins.

3 We are overwhelmed by our faults;
it is you who pardon them.

4 Blessed are those you choose
and bring to reside in your courts.
May we be filled with the blessings of your house,
the holy things of your Temple!

5 With marvelous deeds of justice you answer us,
O God, our Savior—
the hope of all the ends of the earth
and of the distant seas.

6 By your power you hold the mountains firm,
you who are armed with might.

7 You calm the roaring of the seas,
the roaring of their waves
and the tumult among nations.

8 Those who live at the ends of the earth
are in awe at your marvels;
you make east and west resound with joy.

9 You have cared for the land and watered it;
greatly you have enriched it.
God's streams are filled;
you have provided the grain.

10 Thus have you prepared the land:
drenching its furrows,
breaking up its clods,
softening it with showers,
blessing its yield.

11 You have crowned the year with your bounty
and with abundant harvest.
12 The fallow meadows overflow,
and gladness clothes the hills.
13 The fields are arrayed with flocks,
and the valleys blanketed with grain.
They shout and sing for joy.

P S A L M   6 6

Thanksgiving

1 Make a joyful sound to God,
all the earth.
2 Sing the glory of God's name;
give glorious praise!
3 Say to God, "How tremendous are your deeds!"
So great is your power
that your enemies cringe before you.
4 All the earth worships you
and sings praise to you,
sings praise to your name.
5 Come and see what God has done:
tremendous are God's deeds.
6 You, God, changed the sea into dry land;
people passed through the river on foot.
Therefore we rejoice in you,
7 who rule with might forever,
whose eyes keep watch on the nations.
Let not the rebellious exalt themselves.
8 Bless our God, O peoples;
let the sound of God's praise be heard.
9 God has kept us among the living
and has not let our feet slip.

10 For you, O God, have tested us;
   you have tried us as silver is tried.
11 You brought us into the net,
   laying a heavy burden on our backs.
12 You let people ride over our heads.
   We went through fire and through water;
   you brought us forth to a spacious place.
13 I will come into your house with burnt offerings;
   I will fulfill the vows
14 that my lips uttered
   and my mouth promised when I was in trouble.
15 I will offer you burnt offerings of fatlings,
   with the smoke of the sacrifice of rams;
   I will make an offering of oxen and goats.
16 Come and hear, all you who fear God,
   and I will tell what the Holy One has done for me.
17 I cried aloud to God,
   with praise on my tongue.
18 If I had cherished iniquity in my heart,
   God would not have listened.
19 But truly God has listened
   and has heard the voice of my prayer.
20 Blessed be God,
   who has not rejected my prayer
   or withheld steadfast love from me!

P S A L M   6 7

Harvest Song

1 God, show your faithfulness, bless us,
   and make your face smile on us!
2 For then the earth will acknowledge your ways,
   and all the nations will know of your power to save.
3 May all the nations praise you, O God;
   may all the nations praise you!

4 Let the nations shout and sing for joy
since you dispense true justice to the world.
You grant strict justice to the peoples;
on earth you guide the nations.
5 Let the nations praise you, God;
let all the nations praise you!
6 The soil has given its harvest;
God, our God, has blessed us.
7 May God continue to bless us;
and let God be feared to the very ends of the earth.

P S A L M   6 8

Praise of God. Israel's Deliverer

1 Let God arise; let all God's enemies be scattered.
Let those who hate God flee.
2 As smoke is driven away, so drive them away;
as wax melts before fire,
let the wicked perish before God!
3 But let the righteous be joyful;
let them exult before God;
let them be jubilant with joy!
4 Sing to God, sing praises to God's name.
Make way for the One who rides upon the clouds.
God's name is Yahweh.
Rejoice and dance for joy.
5 Father of the fatherless, mother of the orphan,
and protector of the weak is God.
6 God gives the forsaken a home in which to dwell
and leads out the prisoners to freedom;
but the rebellious dwell in a parched land.
7 O God, when you went forth before your people,
when you marched through the wilderness.

8 the earth quaked,
   the heavens poured down rain at your presence.
   Sinai quaked at your presence, O God.
9 Rain in abundance, O God, you shed abroad;
   you restored your heritage as it languished.
10 Your flock found a dwelling;
   in your goodness, O God, you provided for the needy.
11 God gives the command;
   great is the host of those who bore the tidings:
12 "The powerful enemies—they flee.
13 Those at home divide the spoil.
   The wings of the dove are covered with silver,
   its pinions with gold.
14 When the Almighty scattered rulers there,
   snow fell on Zalmon."
15 O mighty mountain, mountain of Bashan;
   O many-peaked mountain, mountain of Bashan!
16 Why look you with jealousy, O many-peaked mountain,
   at the mount where God has chosen to abide,
   where the Most High will dwell forever?
17 With mighty chariots, twice ten thousand,
   thousands upon thousands,
   you came from Sinai into the holy place.
18 You ascended the high mount leading the captives
   and receiving gifts among people—
   even among the rebellious.
   You enter your dwelling.
19 Blessed be God, our Savior,
   who bears our burdens day after day.
20 Our God is a God of salvation;
   and to God belong the keys of death.
21 But God will shatter the heads of all enemies,
   the hairy crowns of those who persist in their guilty ways.
22 God said, "I will bring them back from Bashan.
   I will fetch them from the depths of the sea
23 for your feet to wade in blood,
   for the tongues of your dogs to have their share of the enemy."

24 Your solemn processions are seen, O God,
the processions of my God into the sanctuary—
25 the singers in front, the minstrels behind,
among them youth playing timbrels:
26 "Bless God in your great congregation,
O you who are of Israel's fountain!"
27 There is Benjamin, the least of the tribes in the lead,
the royalty of Judah in their throng,
the royalty of Zebulun, the royalty of Naphtali.
28 Rouse your power, O God;
show your strength, as in the past.
29 Because of your Temple at Jerusalem,
rulers bear gifts to you.
30 Rebuke the beast that dwells among the reeds,
the herd of bulls, the peoples like calves.
Trample under foot those who lust after tribute;
scatter the nations who delight in war.
31 Let bronze be brought from Egypt;
let Ethiopia hasten to stretch out its hands to God.
32 Sing to God, O nations of the earth;
sing praises to the Most High,
33 who rides in the heavens, the ancient heavens.
God sends forth a voice, a mighty voice.
34 Declare the power of God,
whose majesty is over Israel,
and whose power is in the skies.
35 Awesome is God in the sanctuary.
The God of Israel gives power and strength to the people.
Blessed be God!

A Cry of Anguish in Great Distress

1 O God, rescue me!
The waters are up to my chin.
2 I am wallowing in quicksand
with no foothold for safety.
I have slipped into deep water;
the waves pound over me.
3 I am exhausted from calling;
my throat is parched.
My eyes are strained with looking for my God.
4 The number of hairs on my head are fewer
than the number of those who hate me without reason.
Wrongful enemies are legion.
How can I restore what I did not steal?
5 God, you know I am a fool;
my faults cannot be hidden from you.
6 Let those who honor you not be ashamed because of me,
O God of hosts.
Let those who seek you not be dismayed because of me,
O God of Israel.
7 I take insults for your sake,
and dishonor covers my face.
8 I have become an outcast to my ancestors,
a foreigner to my family.
9 Zeal for your house consumes me.
The insults of blasphemers fall upon me.
10 By fasting I humbled myself,
but this was used to reproach me.
11 My garment was sackcloth,
but I was laughed at by all.
12 Those who lounge at the city's gate gossip about me,
and I am the subject of drunkards' songs.

13 As for me, I pray to you
for the time of your favor, O God!
In your faithful love and with your constant help,
answer me.

14 Rescue me from this swamp; let me sink no longer!
Deliver me from my foes.
Save me from the deep waters.

15 Do not let the flood overwhelm me,
nor the abyss swallow me up,
nor the pit close its mouth over me.

16 Your faithful love is abundant;
answer me, O God.

17 Do not conceal your face from your servant;
make haste to answer me in my distress.

18 Come and ransom my life;
redeem me as a rebuke to my enemies.

19 You know the reproach, shame, and disgrace
heaped on me by my foes.

20 Insults have broken my heart.
I am helpless.
I looked for sympathy, but there was none.

21 Instead they fed me poison,
and in my thirst gave me vinegar to drink.

22 Let their own table be a snare and a trap for them.

23 Let their eyes grow dim and then blind,
and afflict their backs with trembling.

24 Pour out your wrath upon them;
let your consuming anger overtake them.

25 Wreck their camp;
tear down their tents.

26 For they torment those you hurt
and add to the pain of those you wound.

27 Heap guilt upon their guilt
and refuse them your reward.

28 Erase their names from the book of the living
and list them not with the names of the just.

29 But I am afflicted and in pain.
Protect me, O God, with your saving help.

30 I will praise your name in song,
   and I will glorify you with thanksgiving—
31 more pleasing to you than oxen,
   or bulls with horns and hooves.
32 "See, humble people, rejoice;
   you who seek God, let your hearts be filled with gladness!
33 For God hears the poor,
   and those in shackles are not spurned by God.
34 Let the heavens and the earth praise God,
   the seas and whatever swims in them!"
35 For God will save Zion
   and rebuild the cities of Judah.
36 They shall dwell in the land and own it,
   and the descendants of God's servants shall inherit it;
   and those who love God's name shall dwell there.

P S A L M   7 0

Prayer of Trust and Appeal

1 O God, make haste to rescue me.
   Come to my aid!
2 Let there be shame and confusion
   on those who seek my life.
   Oh, let them turn back in confusion
   who delight in my harm.
3 Let them retreat, covered with shame,
   who desire my ruin.
4 But let there be rejoicing and gladness
   for all who seek you.
   May those who love your saving help say forever,
   "God is great."
5 As for me, I am needy and poor;
   come to me, O God.
   You are my deliverer and my help.
   O God, do not delay.

An Old Person's Prayer

1 In you, Yahweh, I take refuge;
   never let me be put to shame.
2 In your justice, free me, deliver me.
   Turn your ear to me and save me!
3 Be a sheltering rock for me,
   and a walled fortress to save me;
   for you are my rock, my stronghold.
4 My God, save me from the hands of the wicked,
   from the grasp of rogue and tyrant!
5 For you alone are my hope.
   Yahweh, I have trusted you since my youth;
6 I have leaned on you since I was born.
   You have been my strength from my mother's womb
   and my constant hope.
7 I have seemed a mystery to many,
   but you are my strong refuge.
8 My mouth is full of your praises,
   filled with your splendor day by day.
9 Do not reject me now that I am old,
   nor forsake me now that my strength is failing,
10 for my enemies are making threats;
   spies plan their conspiracy.
11 They say: "God has forsaken you. We will pursue you,
   for there is no one to rescue you."
12 O God, do not be far away.
   My God, come quickly and help me!
13 Shame and ruin on those who attack me;
   may insult and disgrace cover those
   whose desire is to hurt me!
14 I promise that, ever hopeful,
   I will praise you more and more.
15 My lips shall declare your justice
   and power to save, all day long.
16 I will speak of the works of Yahweh,
   commemorate your justice, yours alone.

17　God, you taught me when I was a child,
　　and I am still proclaiming your marvels.
18　I am old, and now my hair is gray.
　　O God, do not forsake me;
　　let me live to tell the next generation
　　about your greatness and power,
19　about your heavenly justice, O God.
　　You have done great things.
　　Who, O God, is like you?
20　You have made me feel misery and hardship,
　　but you will give me life again.
　　You will pull me up again from the depths of the earth,
21　prolong my old age, and once more comfort me.
22　I promise I will praise you on the lyre
　　for your faithfulness, O my God.
　　I will play the harp in your honor,
　　Holy One of Israel.
23　My lips shall sing for joy as I play to you,
　　I whom you have redeemed.
24　And all day long my tongue
　　shall be talking of your justice.
　　Shame and disgrace on those
　　whose aim is to hurt me!

PSALM 72

The Reign of the Messiah

1　O God, with your judgment and with your justice,
　　endow the leaders.
2　They shall govern your people with justice
　　and your afflicted ones with righteousness.
3　The mountains will bring peace for the people,
　　and the hills justice.

4 They shall defend the afflicted among the people,
  save the children of the poor,
  and crush the oppressor.
5 May they endure as long as the sun
  and like the moon through all generations.
6 They shall be like rain coming down on the field,
  like showers watering the earth.
7 Virtue shall flower in their days,
  and world peace till the moon is no more.
8 May they rule from sea to sea,
  and from the river to the ends of the earth.
9 Their foes shall bow before them,
  and their enemies will lick the dust.
10 Tarshish and the Isles shall offer gifts;
   Arabia and Seba shall bring tribute.
11 All other rulers shall pay homage to them,
   all nations shall serve them.
12 For they shall rescue the poor when they cry out
   and the afflicted when they have no one to help them.
13 They shall have pity for the needy and the poor;
   they shall save the lives of the poor.
14 From oppression and violence they shall redeem them,
   and precious shall their blood be.
15 To them, long life and continuous prayers,
   day by day shall they be blessed.
16 May grain be in abundance on the earth,
   and on the tops of the mountains
   the crops shall rustle like Lebanon.
   The city dwellers shall flourish
   like the grass of the fields.
17 Blessed be their name forever;
   their name shall remain as long as the sun.
   In them shall all the nations of the earth be blessed;
   all the nations shall proclaim their happiness.

18 Blessed be Yahweh, the God of Israel,
who alone does wondrous deeds.

19 And blessed forever be God's glorious name;
may the whole earth be filled with God's glory.
Amen. Amen.

PSALM 73

The Triumph of Justice

1 God is indeed good to Israel,
to the pure in heart.

2 But my feet were almost stumbling;
my steps had nearly slipped,

3 because I was jealous of the boasters
and begrudged the wealth of the wicked.

4 There is no such thing as pain for them;
their bodies are healthy and strong.

5 They do not suffer as others do;
no human misery for them!

6 So pride is their chain of honor,
violence the robe that adorns them.

7 Their malice oozes like grease;
their hearts overflow with schemes.

8 They scoff and speak evil;
arrogantly they talk of oppression.

9 They think their mouth is heaven
and their tongue can dictate on earth.

10 This is why my people turn to them
and sip up all they say,

11 asking, "How will God find out?
Does the Most High know everything?

12 Look at them: these are the wicked,
well-off and still they increase in riches."

13 After all, why should I keep my own heart pure
  and wash my hands in innocence
14 if you plague me all day long
  and discipline me every morning?
15 Had I said, "What they say is appealing,"
  I should have betrayed your children.
16 Instead, I worried over the question,
  difficult though I found it—
17 until I solved the mystery
  and saw the end they had in store.
18 They are on a slippery slope,
  placed there by you
  and urged on to ruin
19 until suddenly they become a wasteland—
  finished, terrified to death.
20 When you wake up, Lord, you shake them off
  like delusions of a dream.
21 When my heart had been growing sour
  and I was pained in my innermost parts,
22 I had been foolish and misunderstood;
  I was like a stupid beast before you.
23 Nevertheless, I waited in your presence;
  you grasped my right hand.
24 Now guide me with your counsel
  and receive me into glory at last.
25 No one else in heaven can attract me;
  I delight in nothing else on earth.
26 My flesh and my heart ache with love,
  my heart's foundation, my own, God forever!
27 Truly, to abandon you is to perish.
  You destroy everyone who is unfaithful;
28 as for me, my joy lies in being close to God.
  I have taken shelter in you,
  continually to proclaim what you have done.

Prayer in Time of National Calamity

1 Have you rejected us forever?
Why, O God?
Why is your fury burning
against the sheep of your pasture?

2 Remember your flock, which you gathered of old,
the people you saved as your inheritance—
Mount Zion, where you live.

3 Step carefully through these utter ruins,
toward all the destruction the enemy has done in the sanctuary.

4 Your foes roar victoriously in your shrine;
they have hung up their banners of triumph.

5 Like people with axes hacking in the forest,

6 they chop at all its panels with hammers and hatchets.

7 They set your sanctuary ablaze;
the place where your name abides they have defiled.

8 In their hearts they said:
"Let us destroy, burn all the shrines of God in this land."

9 Without signs on our behalf, or prophets to guide us,
none of us knows how long this will last.

10 How much longer, O God, will the enemy blaspheme?
Will they slander your name forever?

11 Why stay your hand
and stop your right hand—idle under your cloak?

12 Yet, God, my protector from times past,
you bring salvation to the earth.

13 You stirred up the sea by your power;
you crushed the heads of the dragons in the waves.

14 You smashed the heads of Leviathan
and made food for the dolphins.

15 You opened the springs and streams;
you raised dry land out of the waters.

16 The day and the night are yours;
you fashioned the sun and the moon.

17 You established the bounds of the land;
summer and winter—you make them.

18 Recall the blaspheming of the enemy, O God,
and how foolish people insulted your name.
19 Do not feed the wild beast with your dove;
do not forget the lives of your afflicted ones.
20 Remember your covenant,
because every part of the land is now filled with violence.
21 Do not let the oppressed retreat in chaos;
give the poor and needy cause to sing your praises.
22 Arise, O God, defend your cause;
do not forget the endless blaspheming of the fool.
23 Recollect the roaring of your foes,
the increasing tumult among your enemies.

P S A L M   7 5

God, the Just Judge

1 We give you thanks, O God; we give you thanks.
Your name is brought very near to us
in the story of your wonderful deeds.
2 You say, "I choose the appointed time
and then I judge all with justice.
3 When the earth quakes with all who live on it,
I make its pillars firm."
4 To the boastful I say, "Boast no more;"
and to the wicked, "Do not raise your proud horns."
5 Lift not your horns against high heaven,
nor speak arrogantly against your Creator.
6 No power from the east or from the west,
no power from the wilderness can raise a person up.
7 For God is judge,
who puts one down and raises up another.

8 In the hand of Yahweh there is a cup;
the wine foams in it, mixed with spice.
Yahweh offers it to everyone for drink,
and all the wicked on earth must drink it down to the dregs.

9 But I will glorify God forever;
I will sing praises to the God of Jacob and Rachel.

10 I will break off the horns of the wicked,
but the horns of the just shall be lifted high.

P S A L M   7 6

Song after Victory

1 God is made known in Judah.
In Israel God's name is great—

2 the One who set up a tent in Jerusalem
and a dwelling place in Zion.

3 It was there Yahweh broke the flashing arrows,
the shield, the sword, the weapons of war.

4 You, Yahweh, are dazzling with light—
more majestic than the everlasting mountains.

5 The defeated warriors sleep in death;
the hands of the soldiers were powerless.

6 At your rebuke,
horse and rider lay stunned.

7 You, you alone are to be feared.
Who shall stand when your anger is roused?

8 You pronounced your sentence from the heavens.
The earth feared and was still

9 when you arose to judge,
to save the afflicted of the earth.

10 People's anger will serve to praise you;
the survivors surround you in joy.

11 Make vows to your God and fulfill them.
   Let all pay tribute to the One who is to be feared,
12 who cuts short the breath of nobility,
   who strikes terror in the rulers of the earth.

PSALM 7 7

Comfort in Time of Distress

1 **I** cried aloud to you, O God;
       I cried, and you heard me.
2 In the day of my distress I sought you, Yahweh,
   and by night I stretched out my hands in prayer.
   I lay sweating and nothing would cool me;
   I refused all comfort.
3 When I remembered you, I groaned;
   as I pondered, darkness came over my spirit.
4 My eyelids would not close;
   I was troubled and I could not speak.
5 My thoughts went back to times long ago;
   I remembered years past.
6 All night long I was in deep distress;
   as I lay thinking, my spirit was sunk in despair.
7 Yahweh, will you reject us forever
   and never again show us your favor?
8 Has your unfailing love now failed us completely?
   Will your promise be unfulfilled?
9 Have you forgotten how to be gracious?
   Have you withheld your compassion in anger?
10 Has your right hand changed?
   Is the arm of the Most High powerless?
11 But then I remember your deeds;
   I recall your wonders in times gone by.
12 I meditate upon your works
   and ponder all that you have done.

13 O God, your way is holy.
What God is so great as our God?

14 You are the God who works wonders;
you have shown the nations your power.

15 With your strong arm you redeemed your people,
the descendants of Jacob and Rachel.

16 The waters saw you, O God;
they saw you and shuddered in anguish;
the ocean was troubled to its depths.

17 The clouds poured down their water, the skies thundered,
your arrows flashed hither and thither.

18 The sound of your thunder was in the whirlwind,
your lightnings lit up the world,
earth trembled and quaked.

19 Your path led through the sea,
your way was through mighty waters,
and no one marked your footsteps.

20 You guide your people like a flock of sheep
under the hand of Moses, Aaron, and Miriam.

P S A L M   7 8

Lessons of Israelite History

1 O my people, hear my teaching;
listen to the words of my mouth.

2 I will open my mouth in a parable.
I will utter things hidden from of old—

3 things we have heard and known,
things our ancestors have declared to us.

4 We will not hide them from their children;
we will tell the generation to come
of your glorious deeds, O God—
your power, and the wonders you have done.

5 You decreed statutes for Jacob
  and established the law in Israel,
  which you commanded our ancestors
  to teach their children

6 so the next generation would know—
  even the children yet to be born—
  and they in turn would tell their children

7 that they should put their trust in God
  and not forget your deeds
  but keep your commands.

8 They would not be like their ancestors—
  a stubborn and rebellious generation,
  whose hearts were not steadfast,
  whose spirits were not faithful to God.

9 The people of Ephraim, though armed with bows,
  retreated on the day of battle;

10 they did not keep your covenant, O God,
   and refused to live by your law.

11 They forgot what you had done,
   the wonders you had shown them.

12 You did wonderful deeds in the sight of their ancestors
   in the land of Egypt, in the region of Zoan.

13 You divided the sea and led them through;
   you made the water stand firm like a wall.

14 You guided them with the cloud by day
   and with light from the fire all night.

15 You split the rocks in the desert
   and gave them water as abundant as the seas;

16 you brought streams out of a rocky crag
   and made water flow down like rivers.

17 But they continued to sin against you,
   rebelling in the wasteland against the Most High.

18 They willfully put God to the test
   by demanding the food they craved.

19 They spoke against you, saying:
   "Can God spread a table in the desert?

20 When Moses struck the rock, water gushed out,
and streams flowed abundantly.
But can God also give us bread
and supply meat for the people?''
21 When you heard them, you were enraged.
Your fire broke out against Jacob,
and your wrath rose against Israel;
22 for they did not believe in you
or trust in your deliverance.
23 Yet you gave a command to the skies above
and opened the doors of the heavens;
24 you rained down manna for the people to eat
and gave them the bread of heaven.
25 They ate the bread of the mighty;
you sent them more than enough food to eat.
26 You stirred up the east wind from the heavens
and led forth the south wind by your power.
27 You rained meat down on them like dust,
birds like sand on the seashore.
28 You made birds fall inside their camp,
all around their tents.
29 They ate until they had more than enough,
for you had given them what they craved.
30 But before they turned from the food they craved—
even while it was still in their mouths—
31 your anger rose against them;
you put to death the strongest among them,
cutting down the young of Israel.
32 In spite of all this, they kept on sinning;
in spite of your wonders, they did not believe.
33 So you ended their days quickly
and their years in sudden destruction.
34 When you slew them, they would seek you;
they eagerly turned to you again.
35 They remembered that God was their rock,
that God Most High was their redeemer.
36 But then they would flatter you with their mouths,
lying to you with their tongues.

37 Their hearts were not loyal to you;
   they were not faithful to your covenant.
38 Yet you were merciful;
   you forgave their sin
   and did not destroy them.
   Time after time you restrained your anger
   and did not stir up your wrath.
39 You remembered that they were but flesh,
   a passing breath that does not return.
40 How often they rebelled against you in the desert
   and grieved you in the wilderness.
41 Again and again they put you to the test;
   they provoked the Holy One of Israel.
42 They did not remember your power—
   the day you redeemed them from the oppressor,
43 the day you displayed your marvelous signs in Egypt,
   your wonders in the region of Zion.
44 You turned their rivers to blood;
   they could not drink from their streams.
45 You sent swarms of flies that devastated them
   and frogs that lay them waste.
46 You gave their crops to the grasshopper,
   their harvest to the locust.
47 You destroyed their vines with hail
   and their sycamores with frost.
48 You gave over their cattle to the hail,
   their livestock to lightning.
49 You unleashed against them your fierce anger,
   your wrath, indignation and hostility—
   a band of destroying messengers.
50 You prepared a path for your anger;
   you did not spare them from death
   but delivered them to the plague.
51 You struck down all the firstborn of Egypt,
   the firstfruits in the tents of Ham.

52 But you brought your people out like a flock
and led them like sheep through the desert.
53 You guided them safely, so they were unafraid,
but the sea covered their enemies.
54 Thus you brought them to the border of your holy land,
to the hill country your right hand had won.
55 You drove out nations before them
and gave their lands to them as an inheritance;
you settled the tribes of Israel in their homes.
56 But they put you to the test
and rebelled against the Most High;
they did not keep your statutes.
57 Like their ancestors they were disloyal and faithless;
they recoiled like a faulty bow.
58 They angered you with their high places;
they aroused your jealousy with their idols.
59 When you heard them, you were very angry
and rejected Israel completely.
60 You abandoned the tabernacle of Shiloh,
the tent you had set up among them.
61 You sent the ark of your strength into captivity,
your glory into the hands of the enemy.
62 You abandoned people to the sword;
you were very angry with your inheritance.
63 Fire consumed their young men,
and their maidens had no wedding songs;
64 their priests were put to the sword,
and their widows sang no dirges.
65 Then you awoke as from sleep,
as one wakes from the stupor of wine.
66 You beat back their enemies
and put them to everlasting disgrace.
67 Then you rejected the tents of Joseph.
You did not choose the tribe of Ephraim;
68 but you chose the tribe of Judah,
Mount Zion, which you loved.
69 You built a sanctuary like the high mountains,
like the earth which you founded forever.

70 You chose David your servant
    and took him from the sheepfolds;
71 from tending the sheep you brought him
    to be the shepherd of the chosen people of Israel.
72 And David shepherded them with integrity of heart,
    guiding them with skillful hands.

P S A L M 7 9

National Lament

1   O God, the nations have invaded your heritage.
    They have defiled your holy Temple;
    they have reduced Jerusalem to ruins.
2   They have left the corpses of your servants
    to the birds of the air for food,
    and the flesh of your faithful ones to the beasts of the earth.
3   They have shed blood like water throughout Jerusalem—
    there is no one left to bury them.
4   We have become a taunt to our neighbors,
    the scorn and laughingstock of all those around us.
5   How much longer will you be angry, Yahweh?
    Forever?
    Is your jealousy to burn like a fire?
6   Turn your anger on the nations who reject you,
    and on those kingdoms
    that do not call on your name,
7   for they have devoured Jacob and Rachel
    and reduced their home to rubble.
8   Do not blame us for the crimes of our ancestors.
    In haste come to our side, for we are brought low.
9   Help us, O God, our Salvation,
    for the glory of your name.
    Yahweh, pardon our sins;
    free us for the sake of your name.

10 Why should the nations demand, "Where is their God?"
    May they soon learn that you avenge
    the taking of your servants' blood.
11 May the sighs of the enslaved reach you.
    By your great power, rescue those doomed to die!
12 Pay our neighbors sevenfold, strike them to the heart
    for the disgrace they inflicted upon you, Yahweh.
13 Then we your people, the flock that you pasture,
    will give you everlasting thanks
    and will recite your praises forever and ever.

P S A L M   8 0

Prayer for the Restoration of Israel

1   **H**ear me, O Shepherd of Israel!
    You who guide Joseph like a flock.
    Enthroned on the cherubs, shine out
2   on Ephraim, Benjamin, and Manasseh.
    Rouse your power and come to save us!
3   Restore us, Yahweh.
    We will be secure when you smile upon us.
4   How long will you be angry, Yahweh,
    while your people pray?
5   We have fed on bread of tears,
    drunk them in ample measure.
6   Our neighbors now argue over us
    and our foes mock us.
7   Yahweh, bring us back.
    Smile on us and we will be secure.
8   From Egypt you uprooted a vine;
    to plant it you scattered other nations.
9   You cleared a space so it could flourish,
    and it took root and filled the land.
10 Soon it shaded the mountains,
    the cedars of God by its branches.

11 Its leaves stretched to the sea,
   its shoots to the river.
12 Why have you leveled its fences?
   Now all can pluck its fruit.
13 The wild boar can trample it,
   and wild beasts devour it.
14 O Yahweh, please return!
   Look down from heaven and see this vine.
15 Nurture and guard what your hand has planted.
16 They tossed it on the flames like rubbish,
   but your glance would destroy them.
17 Safeguard those you have chosen,
   those you have made strong.
18 Never again will we turn away from you;
   we shall call on your holy name with a renewed spirit.
19 Restore us, Yahweh Sabaoth;
   let your face smile on us—
   then we will be safe.

PSALM 81

A Festive Song and a Call to Fidelity

1 Sing out in praise of God our strength,
   acclaim the God of Jacob and Rachel.
2 Take pipe and timbrel;
   take tuneful harp and lyre.
3 Blow the trumpet for the new month,
   for the full moon on the day of our pilgrim-feast.
4 For this is a law for Israel,
   a decree of the God of Abraham and Sarah,
5 laid as a solemn charge on Joseph
   when he came out of Egypt.
6 When I lifted the burden from your shoulders,
   your hands were freed from the builder's basket.

7   When you cried to me in distress, I rescued you;
      unseen, I answered you in thunder.
      I tested you at the waters of Meribah,
8   where I opened wide your mouths and filled them.
      I fed Israel with the finest wheat flour
      and satisfied you with honey from the rocks.
9   Listen, my people, while I admonish you.
      Listen to me, O Israel:
10 You shall have no strange god among you
      nor bow down to any foreign god.
11 I am Yahweh, your God,
      who brought you up from Egypt.
12 But my people did not listen to my voice,
      and Israel would not obey me;
13 so I sent them off, stubborn as they were,
      to follow their own way.
14 If only my people would listen to me,
      if Israel would only walk in my ways,
15 I would soon humble their enemies
      and lay a heavy hand upon their persecutors.
16 Let those who hate me come cringing before me
      and meet with everlasting troubles.

P S A L M 8 2

Judgment against Wicked Judges

1   **G**od arises in the divine assembly
      and judges in the midst of the gods:
2   "How long will you defend the unjust
      and favor the cause of the wicked?"
3   Defend the poor and the orphaned;
      render justice to the afflicted and the oppressed.
4   Rescue the lowly and the poor;
      from the clutches of the wicked deliver them.

5 They have neither knowledge nor understanding—
  they walk about blindly.
  All the order of the world is shaken.
6 I said: "You are gods,
  all of you.
7 Yet like mortals you shall die—
  fall like any ruler."
8 Rise, O God; judge the earth,
  for yours are all the nations.

P S A L M   8 3

Prayer against a Hostile Alliance

1 **O** God, do not be silent;
  do not hold your peace or keep still, O God!
2 For your enemies raise a ruckus;
  those who hate you have stuck up their heads.
3 They plot crafty deeds against your people;
  they conspire together against your protected ones.
4 They say, "Come, let us destroy them as a nation;
  let the name of Israel be remembered no more!"
5 Yes, they conspire with one accord;
  against you they are allied:
6 the tents of Edom and the Ishmaelites,
  Moab and the Hagrites,
7 Gebal and Ammon and Amalek,
  Philistia with the inhabitants of Tyre;
8 Assyria also has joined them;
  they are the strong arm of the children of Lot.
9 Do to them as you did to Midian,
  as to Sisera and Jabin at the river Kishon,
10 who were destroyed at Endor,
  who became dung for the ground.
11 Make their nobles like Oreb and Zeeb,
  all their people like Zebah and Zalmunna,

12 who said, "Let us take possession
    of the dwelling place of God for ourselves."
13 O my God, make them like whirling dust,
    like leaves in the wind.
14 As fire consumes the forest—
    as the flame sets the mountains ablaze—
15 so do you pursue them with your tempest
    and terrify them with your storm!
16 Fill their faces with shame
    that they may seek your name.
17 Let them be put to shame and dismayed forever;
    let them perish in disgrace.
18 Let them know that you alone are God,
    whose name is the Most High over all the earth.

PSALM 84

Pilgrimage Song

1 How I love your dwelling place,
    Yahweh Sabaoth!
2 How my soul yearns and pines for your courts!
    My heart and my flesh cry out to you, the living God.
3 Finally, the sparrow has found its home,
    the swallow a nest for its young—
    your altars, Yahweh Sabaoth, O my God.
4 Happy those who dwell in your house
    and praise you all day long.
5 Happy those whose strength is in you;
    they have courage to make the pilgrimage!

6   As they go through the Valley of the Weeper,
     they make it a place of springs,
     clothed in generous growth by early rains.
7   They make their way from strength to strength,
     soon to see God in Zion.
8   Yahweh Sabaoth, hear my prayer;
     listen, God of Jacob and Rebekah.
9   Now look on us, God our Shield,
     and be kind to your anointed.
10   Only one day in your courts
     is worth more than a thousand elsewhere;
     merely to stand at the door of God's house
     is better than living with the wicked.
11   For you, God, are a sun and shield,
     bestowing grace and glory.
     Yahweh withholds nothing good
     from those who walk without blame.
12   Yahweh Sabaoth, happy those who put their trust in you.

P S A L M   8 5

The Coming Age of Peace and Justice

1   Yahweh, you have favored your land
     and restored the well-being of Israel;
2   you have forgiven the guilt of your people
     and covered all their sins.
3   You set aside all your rage;
     you calmed the heat of your anger.
4   Restore us now, God, our Savior!
     Put an end to your displeasure with us.
5   Will you be angry with us forever?
     Will your anger never cease?
6   Will you not instead restore our life
     that your people may rejoice in you?

7 Let us see your faithfulness
   and give us your saving help.
8 I will hear what you, God, proclaim:
   a voice that speaks of peace—
   peace for your faithful
   and those who turn to you in hope.
9 Your salvation is near for those who fear you,
   and your glory will dwell in our land.
10 Love and faithfulness have met;
   justice and peace have embraced.
11 Faithfulness shall spring from the earth
   and justice look down from heaven.
12 Yahweh, you will give what is good,
   and our earth shall yield its fruit.
13 Justice shall march before you,
   and peace shall follow your steps.

PSALM 86

A Prayer for Help

1 Listen to me, O God, and answer me,
   because I am poor and afflicted.
2 Save me from death, because I am loyal to you;
   save me, because I am your servant and trust in you.
3 You are my God, so be merciful to me.
   I call to you all day long.
4 Make your servant glad,
   because I lift my soul to you.
5 Yahweh, you are good and forgiving,
   full of faithful love for all who pray to you.
6 Listen to my prayer;
   hear my cry for help.

7 I call to you in times of trouble,
for you answer my prayer.
8 There is no other god like you, Yahweh—
not one who can do the deeds you do.
9 All the nations you have created
will come and worship you.
They will praise your greatness
10 because only you, God, are mighty;
only you do wonderful deeds.
11 Teach me your way, Yahweh,
and I will obey you faithfully;
give me an undivided heart
that I may fear your name.
12 I will praise you with all my heart, O my God;
I will proclaim your greatness forever.
13 Great is your faithful love for me!
You have saved me from the depths of the grave.
14 God, the arrogant are coming against me,
a cruel gang is trying to kill me,
people who have no regard for you.
15 Yahweh, you are a compassionate and loving God,
slow to anger, always kind and faithful.
16 Turn to me and have mercy on me;
strengthen me and save me
because I serve you just as my mother and father did.
17 Show me proof of your goodness, Yahweh;
then those who hate me will be ashamed
when they see that you have given me comfort and help.

P S A L M   8 7

Zion, Home of Nations

1   **Y**ahweh loves this city
    founded on the holy mountain—
2   preferring the gates of Zion
    to any dwelling of Jacob.
3   And Yahweh has glorious things to say of you,
    city of God!
4   ''I will tell of Egypt and Babylon
    to the nations that know me.
    Of Philistia, Tyre, Ethiopia,
    people say, 'Here so and so was born.'
5   But Zion is called 'Mother,'
    since all were born in her.''
    It is Yahweh who has established her—
7   And all shall sing and dance!
    All find their home in you.

P S A L M   8 8

Lament

1   **Y**ahweh, my God, I call for help all day;
    I cry out to you all night.
2   May my prayer come to you.
    Hear my cries for help,
3   for my soul is troubled;
    my life draws near to Sheol.
4   I am counted among those
    who, without strength, go down to the pit.
5   I am alone, down among the dead,
    among the slain in their graves—
    among those you have forgotten,
    those deprived of your care.

6 You have plunged me to the bottom of the pit,
into its very bottom.
7 I am crushed by your anger,
drowned beneath your waves.
8 You have turned my friends against me
and made me a pariah to them.
I am in prison and unable to escape,
9 my eyes exhausted with suffering.
Yahweh, I call to you all day;
to you I stretch out my hands.
10 Are your wonders meant for the dead?
Can they rise up to praise you?
11 Who proclaims your love from the grave,
your faithfulness among those who have died?
12 Are your wonders discussed in the dark,
your justice in the land of oblivion?
13 But I am here, pleading for your help,
waiting for you every morning.
14 O God, why do you reject me?
Why do you hide your face from me?
15 I am afflicted and have suffered since my youth;
I bore your fury; now I almost despair.
16 Your anger overwhelmed me;
you shattered me with your terrors,
17 which, like a flood, engulfed me all day long—
all together closing in on me.
18 You have turned my friends and neighbors against me;
now darkness is my only friend.

PSALM 89

A Hymn of God's Faithfulness

1   **I** will sing the wonders of your love forever, Yahweh;
    I will proclaim your faithfulness to all generations.

2   I will declare that your love is steadfast,
    your faithfulness fixed as the heavens.*

5   The heavens praise your wonders, Yahweh,
    and the assembly of the holy ones exalts your faithfulness.

6   In the skies who is there like Yahweh?
    Who is like the One in the court of heaven,

7   like God who is feared among the assembled holy ones,
    great and awesome above all?

8   O God of Hosts, who is like you?
    Your strength and faithfulness surround you.

9   You rule the surging sea,
    calming the turmoil of its waves.

10 You crush the monster Rahab with a mortal blow
    and scatter your enemies with your strong arm.

11 Yours are the heavens; the earth is yours also.
    You founded the world with all that is in it.

12 You created north and south;
    Tabor and Hermon echo your name.

13 Strength of arm and power are yours.
    Your hand is mighty, your right hand lifted high.

14 Your throne is built upon righteousness and justice;
    true love and faithfulness herald your coming.

15 Happy the people who have learned to acclaim you,
    who walk in the light of your presence!

16 In your name they shall rejoice all day long;
    your righteousness shall lift them up.

17 You are their strength and glory;
    and by your favor we hold our heads high.

18 Yahweh is our shield;
    the Holy One of Israel is our ruler.

*Verses 3 and 4 have been moved to follow verse 19.

19 Then you announced in a vision
and declared to your faithful servants:

3   I have made a covenant with the one I have chosen;
I have sworn to my servant David:

4   I will establish his posterity forever,
I will make his throne firm for all generations.
The youth I have chosen towers over the people.

20 I have found David my servant:
I have anointed him with my holy oil.

21 My hand shall be ready to help him,
and my arm to give him strength.

22 No enemy shall strike at him
and no rebel bring him low;

23 I will shatter his foes before him
and crush those who hate him.

24 My faithfulness and true love shall be with him,
and through my name he shall hold his head high.

25 I will extend his rule over the sea
and his dominion as far as the river.

26 He will say to me, "You are my God,
my rock, and my safe refuge."

27 And I will name him my firstborn,
highest among the people of the earth.

28 I will maintain my love for him forever
and be faithful in my covenant with him.

29 I will make his posterity last forever
and his throne as long as the heavens endure.

30 If his descendants forsake my law
and do not conform to my judgments,

31 if they renounce my statutes
and do not observe my commands,

32 I will punish their disobedience with the rod
and their iniquity with lashes.

33 Yet I will not deprive him of my true love
nor let my faithfulness prove false;

34 I will not renounce my covenant
nor change my promise.

35 I have sworn by my holiness once and for all;
I will not break my word.

36   His posterity shall continue forever,
       his throne shall be like the sun before me,

37   it shall be sure forever
       as the moon that remains forever faithful
       as long as the skies remain.

38 Yet you have rejected David
   and you have spurned and raged against the anointed.

39 You have denounced the covenant with your servant,
   defiled the crown and flung it to the ground.

40 You have broken the walls
   and laid the strongholds in ruin.

41 All who pass by plunder the anointed
   who suffers the taunts of neighbors.

42 You have increased the power of the enemies
   and brought joy to all the foes.

43 You have let the sharp sword be driven back
   without help in the battle.

44 You have put an end to the glorious rule
   and hurled the throne to the ground.

45 You have cut short youth and vigor
   and covered the anointed with shame.

46 How long, O God, will you hide yourself from sight?
   How long must your wrath blaze like fire?

47 Remember that I shall not live forever.
   How frail you created humanity.

48 Who shall live and not see death
   or save themselves from the power of Sheol?

49 Where are the former acts of your love, O God—
   those faithful promises given to David?

50 Remember the insults hurled at your servant,
   how I have borne in my heart the accusations of the nations.

51 So have your enemies taunted us, O God,
   taunted the successors of your anointed one.

52 Blessed is God forever.
   Amen. Amen.

Pondering on the Brevity of Life

1   **Y**ahweh, you have been my security
      from generation after generation.
2   Before the mountains were formed
      or the earth was born,
      you are God, without beginning or end.
3   You turn humans into dust and command:
      "Go back."
4   A thousand years are like yesterday to you—
      come and gone—
      no more than a moment in the night.
5   You sweep humans away like daydreams,
      like fresh grass which springs up
6   and flowers in the morning,
      but by evening is withered and dry.
7   We are consumed by your anger,
      in terror of your fury.
8   We stare at our guilt and our secrets
      made clear in the light of your face.
9   All our days pass away in your anger;
      our lives are over in a sigh.
10   Seventy years is our life span,
      or eighty for those who are strong.
      These years are painful and empty.
11   Who comprehends the force of your wrath
      and trembles at the strength of your fury?
12   Make us realize the shortness of life
      that we may gain wisdom of heart.
13   Yahweh, relent! Is your anger forever?
      Have mercy on your servants.
14   When morning comes, fill us with your love.
      And then we shall celebrate all our days.

15 Balance our afflictions with joy;
    for years we only knew misfortune.
16 Show your servants what you do for them;
    may your glory shine on their children.
17 May the goodness of Yahweh be upon us!
    Grant success to the work of our hands.

P S A L M   9 1

Security under God's Protection

1 You who dwell in the shelter of the Most High,
   who abide in the shadow of the Almighty,
2 say: "My Refuge and my Strength,
   my God in whom I trust."
3 For God will save you from the snare of the fowler,
   from the destroying pestilence.
4 With pinions God will cover you,
   and under God's wings you shall find refuge;
   God's faithfulness is a guard and a shield.
5 You will not fear the terror of the night
   nor the arrow that flies by day;
6 not the pestilence that stalks in darkness
   nor the plague that destroys at noon.
7 Though a thousand fall at your side,
   ten thousand at your right side,
   you will remain secure.
8 Behold, look with your own eyes
   and see the punishment of the wicked—
9 because you have God for your refuge.
   You have made the Most High your stronghold.
10 No harm shall befall you,
   nor shall affliction come near your tent;
11 God has commanded angels
   to guard you in all your ways.

12   In their hands they shall raise you up
     so that you will not hurt your foot against a stone.

13   You shall tread upon the lion and the viper;
     you shall trample the lion and the dragon.

14   "Because you cling to me, I will deliver you;
     I will protect you because you acknowledge my name.

15   You shall call upon me and I will answer you.
     I will be with you in times of trouble;
     I will deliver you and glorify you
     and will show you my salvation."

P S A L M   9 2

The Virtuous Rejoice

1   O Yahweh, it is good to give you thanks,
     to sing psalms to your name, O Most High;

2   to declare your love in the morning
     and your faithfulness every night,

3   with the music of a ten-stringed lute,
     to the melody of the harp.

4   Your acts, O Yahweh, fill me with gladness;
     I shout in triumph at your mighty deeds.

5   How great are your deeds, Yahweh!
     How deep are your thoughts!

6   Those who do not know this are senseless,
     fools are they who do not understand this:

7   that though the wicked grow like grass
     and every evildoer flourishes,
     they will be destroyed forever.

8   But you, Yahweh, are exalted forever,
     your foes will surely perish,

9   all evildoers will be scattered.

10   I lift my head high, like a wild ox tossing its horns;
     I am anointed with fine oils.

11 I see the defeat of my enemies;
   I listen for the downfall of my cruel foes.
12 The just flourish like a palm tree,
   they grow tall as a cedar of Lebanon.
13 Planted as they are in the house of the Creator,
   they flourish in the courts of our God,
14 bearing fruit in old age like trees full of sap—
   vigorous, wide-spreading—
15 eager to declare that Yahweh is just,
   my Rock, in whom there is no wrong.

P S A L M   9 3

The Glory of God

1 O God, you reign;
   you are robed in splendor and clothed with strength.
   The world is firmly established;
   it cannot be moved.
2 Your throne has stood since long ago;
   you are everlasting.
3 The seas have lifted up, O Yahweh,
   the seas have lifted up their voice;
   the seas have lifted up their pounding waves.
4 More powerful than the thunder of the great waters,
   mightier than the breakers of the sea—
   Yahweh is powerful on high.
5 Your decrees stand firm;
   holiness adorns your house
   for endless days.

God, the Judge of All

1   O God, you are a God who punishes;
    you reveal your anger!
2   You are the judge of all the earth.
    Rise and give the proud what they deserve!
3   How much longer will the wicked be glad?
    How much longer?
4   How much longer will evildoers be proud
    and boast about their crimes?
5   They trample your people, God;
    they oppress those who belong to you.
6   They kill the weak and orphans
    and murder the strangers who live in our land.
7   They say, "Yahweh does not see us;
    the God of Israel does not notice!"
8   My people, you senseless fools,
    when will you be wise?
9   Cannot God who made our ears, hear?
    The One who made our eyes, see?
10 Will not God who disciplines the nations
    punish them?
    Does not God who is the teacher of all
    have knowledge?
11 God knows their thoughts
    and knows how senseless their reasoning is.
12 Yahweh, happy are those you instruct,
    those you teach by your law.
13 You give them rest from days of trouble,
    until a grave is dug for the wicked.
14 Yahweh will not abandon the people
    and will never desert those who belong to the covenant.
15 Justice will again be found in courts of judgment,
    and all righteous people will support it.
16 Who stood up for me against the wicked?
    Who took my side against the evildoers?

17 If Yahweh had not helped me,
   I would have gone quickly to a silent grave.

18 I said, "I am falling";
   but Yahweh, your faithful love supported me.

19 When I am anxious and worried,
   you comfort me and make me glad.

20 You have nothing to do with corrupt judges
   who make injustice legal,

21 who plot against the good
   and sentence the innocent to death.

22 Yet Yahweh is my stronghold,
   and God my Rock of Refuge
   defends and protects me.

23 God will punish them for their wickedness
   and destroy them for their sins;
   our God will destroy them.

P S A L M   9 5

A Call to Praise and Obedience

1 Come, let us sing joyfully to God;
   let us acclaim the Rock of our salvation.

2 Let us greet God with thanksgiving;
   let us joyfully sing psalms.

3 For Yahweh is a great God
   above all gods;

4 God cradles the depths of the earth
   and holds fast the mountain peaks.

5 God shaped the sea and owns it
   and formed the dry land by hand.

6 Come, let us bow down in worship;
   let us kneel before the God who made us.

7 For Yahweh is our God,
   and we are the people God shepherds,
   the flock God leads.
   O that today you would hear God's voice:
8 "Do not harden your hearts as at Meribah.
   as on that day in the desert of Massah
9 where your ancestors challenged me;
   they tested me though they had seen my works.
10 Forty years with that generation,
   and I said: They are a people of
   erring heart and they know not my ways.
11 Therefore I swore in my anger:
   They shall not enter into my rest."

P S A L M   9 6

The Glory of God

1 **S**ing Yahweh a new song!
   Sing to Yahweh, you lands!
2 Sing to Yahweh; bless God's name.
   Proclaim God's salvation day after day.
3 Tell God's glory among the nations;
   tell God's wondrous deeds to all people.
4 For Yahweh is great; loud must be God's praise.
   Yahweh is to be feared above all gods.
5 All the gods of the nations are as nothing.
   Yahweh created the heavens;
6 splendor and majesty are in God's presence,
   power and beauty in God's sanctuary.
7 Families of the nations give all honor to Yahweh,
   give glory and praise to God.
8 Bring gifts; bear them before God.
9 Worship Yahweh in the sacred court;
   tremble before Yahweh, all the earth!

10 Say among the nations, "Yahweh is our Rock!"
Yahweh has made the world unshakable;
Yahweh will judge each nation with equity.

11 Let the heavens be glad, and the earth rejoice;
let the sea and all that it holds resound.

12 Let the fields and all that is in them exult;
let all the forests cry out for joy

13 at the presence of Yahweh, for God comes
to judge the earth,
to judge the world with justice
and the nations with truth.

P S A L M   9 7

The Just Judge

1 Yahweh, you reign! Let the earth rejoice;
let the many coastlands be glad!

2 Clouds and thick darkness are round about you;
righteousness and justice
are the foundation of your throne.

3 Fire goes before you consuming your foes.

4 Your lightning illumines the world;
the earth sees and trembles.

5 The mountains melt like wax before you,
before the God of all the earth.

6 The heavens proclaim your justice,
and all the nations behold your glory.

7 All idol worshipers are put to shame,
who make their boast in worthless idols;
all gods bow down before you.

8 Zion hears and is glad,
and the cities of Judah rejoice
because of your judgments, O God.

9 For you, Yahweh, are most high over all the earth;
you are raised far above all gods.

10 You, Yahweh, love those who hate evil;
   you protect the lives of your faithful ones
   and deliver them from the grasp of the wicked.
11 Light dawns for the just,
   and joy for the upright in heart.
12 Rejoice in Yahweh, O you just,
   and give thanks to God's holy name!

PSALM 98

Orchestra of Praise to God

1   **S**ing a new song to Yahweh,
      who has done wonderful deeds,
    whose right hand and whose holy arm
    have brought salvation.
2   Yahweh has made salvation known,
    has shown justice to the nations,
3   and has remembered the house of Israel
    in faithfulness and love.
    All the ends of the earth have seen
    the saving power of our God.
4   Sing praise to Yahweh all the earth;
    ring out your joy.
5   Sing psalms to Yahweh with the harp,
    with the sound of music.
6   With trumpets and the sound of the horn,
    acclaim Yahweh.
7   Let the sea and all within it resound,
    the world and all its peoples.
8   Let the rivers clap their hands
    and the mountains ring out their joy
9   at the presence of the Just Judge who comes,
    who comes to rule the earth.
    Yahweh will rule the world with justice
    and the peoples with fairness.

The Holy One

1 **Y**ahweh rules; the nations tremble.
      Yahweh is enthroned on the cherubs;
   the earth quakes.
2 Yahweh is great in Zion.
   Yahweh, you are high above all nations.
3 May they praise your great and awesome name.
4 Holy are you and mighty!
   You are a God who loves justice,
   insisting on goodness, justice, and honesty
   as you have done for Jacob and Rebekah.
5 Let us extol Yahweh, our God.
   Holy is God!
6 Moses and Miriam, Aaron and Samuel, all invoked Yahweh;
   and God answered them.
7 Yahweh spoke with them in the pillar of cloud;
   they did God's will and kept the law God gave them.
8 Yahweh, our God, you answered them;
   you are a God of forgiveness
   though punishing them for their sins.
9 Extol Yahweh, our God;
   worship at God's holy mountain,
   for holy is Yahweh, our God!

An Invitation to Praise God

1 **S**hout for joy to God,
      all the lands!
2 Serve God with gladness!
   Come into God's presence with joyful singing!

3 Know that Yahweh is God!
   Yahweh made us, and we belong to God;
   we are God's people and the sheep of God's pasture.
4 Enter God's gates with thanksgiving
   and the courts with praise!
   Give thanks to God; bless God's name!
5 For Yahweh is good;
   God's steadfast love endures forever,
   and God's faithfulness to all generations.

P S A L M   1 0 1

The Ideal Ruler

1 **M**y song is about faithfulness and justice;
   Yahweh, I sing it to you.
2 I will walk in the way of integrity.
   When will you come to me?
   In my household I will walk with a blameless heart.
3 I will not let my eyes rest on any evil deed.
   I hate those who act perversely;
   they shall be far from me.
4 Crooked hearts must keep their distance.
   I avoid the wicked.
5 Those who secretly slander their neighbor
   I will silence;
   I cannot endure haughty looks or proud hearts.
6 I look to those who are faithful
   to dwell in my household;
   only those who walk in integrity, as the blameless do,
   can be my servants.

7 There is no space in my abode
   for those who practice deceit;
   no liars will stand in my presence.
8 Morning after morning I silence
   all who are wicked in this country,
   uprooting from the city of Yahweh all evil ones.

P S A L M   1 0 2

Prayer in Misfortune

1 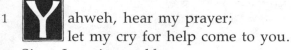ahweh, hear my prayer;
   let my cry for help come to you.
2 Since I am in trouble,
   do not conceal your face from me.
   Turn and listen to me.
   When I call, respond to me quickly.
3 For my days are vanishing like smoke,
   my bones burn like fire,
4 my heart withers like scorched grass;
   even my appetite is gone.
5 And when I sigh,
   my skin clings to my bones.
6 I am like a pelican living in the wilderness,
   or a screech owl haunting the ruins.
7 I lie awake moaning
   like some lonely bird on the rooftops.
8 All day long my enemies insult me,
   and those who used to respect me
   use my name like a curse.
9 The bread I eat has become like ashes;
   what I drink is mixed with my tears—
   all because of your anger.
10 You lifted me up so you could throw me back down.
11 My days pass away like shadows;
   I wither away like grass.

12 But you, Yahweh, endure forever;
    every age remembers you!
13 Rise! Forgive Zion!
    Pity Zion, for it is time—
    at last the hour has come.
14 Your servants love even Zion's stones
    and are moved to pity by the city's dust.
15 Then the nations will revere your name, Yahweh,
    and all the rulers on earth will respect your glory
16 when you found Zion anew
    and then appear in glory.
17 Yahweh, you will answer the prayer of the helpless
    and will not laugh at their plea.
18 Record this for future generations
    so that people not born yet can praise God.
19 Yahweh has leaned down from the sanctuary's heights,
    and has gazed down at earth from the heavens
20 to hear the groans of the prisoners
    and to liberate those doomed to die.
21 The children of your servants will have a home,
    and their descendants will dwell in your presence forever
    to praise your name in Jerusalem.
22 Nations will be united—
    offering worship to Yahweh together.
23 My strength is broken;
    my days are cut short.
24 Do not take me away in the midst of my days,
    when your own life lasts forever.
25 In the beginning you laid the earth's foundations;
    the heavens are the work of your hands.
26 They will perish, though you remain—
    they will wear out like a garment.
    As clothes are changed,
    so will you change them.
27 But you remain the same,
    and your years will never end.

PSALM 103

God Is Love

1 Bless Yahweh, O my soul.
Bless God's holy name, all that is in me!
2 Bless Yahweh, O my soul,
and remember God's faithfulness:
3 in forgiving all your offenses,
in healing all your diseases,
4 in redeeming your life from destruction,
in crowning you with love and compassion,
5 in filling your years with good things,
in renewing your youth like an eagle's.
6 Yahweh does justice
and always takes the side of the oppressed.
7 God's ways were revealed to Moses,
and Yahweh's deeds to Israel.
8 Yahweh is merciful and forgiving,
slow to anger, rich in love;
9 Yahweh's wrath does not last forever;
it exists a short time only.
10 We are never threatened, never punished
as our guilt and our sins deserve.
11 As the height of heaven over earth
is the greatness of Yahweh's faithful love
for those who fear God.
12 Yahweh takes our sins away
farther than the east is from the west.
13 As tenderly as parents treat their children,
so Yahweh has compassion on those who fear God.
14 Yahweh knows what we are made of;
Yahweh remembers that we are dust.
15 The human lasts no longer than grass,
lives no longer than a flower in the field.
16 One gust of wind, and that one is gone,
never to be seen there again.

17 But Yahweh's faithful love for those who fear God
   lasts from all eternity and forever,
   so too God's justice to their children's children,
18 as long as they keep the covenant
   and remember to obey its precepts.
19 Yahweh has established a throne in the heavens
   and rules over all.
20 Bless Yahweh, all angels,
   mighty in strength to enforce God's word,
   attentive to every command.
21 Bless Yahweh, all nations,
   servants who do God's will.
22 Bless Yahweh, all creatures
   in every part of the world.
   Bless Yahweh, O my soul.

P S A L M   1 0 4

The Glories of Creation

1 Bless Yahweh, O my soul.
   How great you are, Yahweh, my God!
   You are clothed in majesty and splendor,
2 wrapped in a robe of light!
   You spread the heavens out like a tent;
3 you build your high walls upon the waters above.
   The clouds are your chariot
   as you travel on the wings of the wind.
4 The breezes are your messengers
   and fiery flames your servants.
5 You fixed the earth on its foundations
   so that it cannot be moved;
6 you cover it with the deep as with a robe,
   the waters enveloping the mountains.
7 At your charge the waters took to flight,
   they fled at the sound of your thunder,

8 pouring over the mountains, settling into the valleys,
   down to the place you made for them.
9 You set a limit they must never cross—
   nor shall they flood the land again.
10 You set springs gushing in ravines,
    flowing between the mountains,
11 giving drink to wild animals,
    drawing the thirsty wild donkeys.
12 The birds of the air make their nests
    and sing among the branches nearby.
13 From your palace you water the hills.
    You fill the earth with the fruit of your works.
14 You make fresh grass grow for cattle,
    and fruit for your people.
    You bring forth food from the earth:
15 wine to make them rejoice,
    oil to make them happy,
    and bread to make them strong.
16 The trees of Yahweh are well watered—
    those cedars of Lebanon.
17 Here the birds build their nest;
    and on the highest branches, the stork has its home.
18 For the wild goats there are the mountains;
    badgers hide in the rocks.
19 You made the moon to mark the seasons;
    the sun knows the hour of its setting.
20 You form the shadows, night falls,
    and all the forest animals prowl about—
21 the lions roar for their prey
    and seek their food from God.
22 At sunrise they retire,
    to lie down in their lairs.
23 People go out to work
    and to labor until the evening.
24 Yahweh, how many are the works you have created,
    arranging everything in wisdom!
    Earth is filled with creatures you have made:
25 see the vast ocean
    teeming with countless creatures, great and small,

26 where ships go to and fro,
  and Leviathan that you made to play for you.
27 All creatures depend on you
  to give them food in due season.
28 You give the food they eat;
  with generous hand, you fill them with good things.
29 If you turn your face away—they suffer;
  if you stop their breath—they die and return to dust.
30 When you give your spirit, they are created.
  You keep renewing the world.
31 Glory forever to you, Yahweh!
  May you find joy in your creation.
32 At your glance the earth trembles;
  at your touch the mountains smoke!
33 All my life I will sing to Yahweh;
  I will play for you, my God, as long as I live.
34 May my life be pleasing to you
  while I find my joy on earth!
35 May sinners vanish from the earth,
  and the wicked exist no more!
  Bless Yahweh, O my soul.

P S A L M   1 0 5

The Wonderful History of Israel

1 Alleluia! Give thanks to Yahweh!
  Praise God's name,
  and make known God's deeds to the nations!
2 Sing to God; sing praise
  and tell of all God's wonderful works.
3 Glory in God's holy name;
  let the hearts that seek Yahweh rejoice!
4 Seek Yahweh—
  constantly seek God's face;

5 remember the marvels accomplished—
   and the judgments from God's mouth.
6 Descendants of Abraham and Sarah, God's servants,
   offspring of Jacob and Rachel, God's chosen ones,
7 Yahweh is our God,
   whose authority is over all the earth.
8 God remembers the covenant forever:
   the promise for a thousand generations,
9 the pact made with Abraham and Sarah,
   the oath to Isaac and Rebekah.
10 Yahweh established it by decree
   as an everlasting covenant for Israel.
11 "I will give you a land," God said,
   "Canaan, your allotted heritage."
12 When they were easily counted,
   few in number, strangers to the country,
13 they went from nation to nation,
   from one kingdom to another people.
14 God let no one oppress them
   and rebuked rulers on their behalf.
15 "Do not touch my anointed," God said;
   "do not harm my prophets!"
16 Then Yahweh called down famine on the country
   and ruined the crop that fed them.
17 God sent ahead of them
   Joseph, sold as a slave.
18 They tortured him with chains;
   they bound him in irons.
19 In time, Joseph's oracle came true,
   and Yahweh's word proved him right.
20 The ruler gave orders to release him.
   That master of nations set him free,

21 placing Joseph in charge of the household,
   ruler of all the leader possessed,
22 to train the officials as Joseph pleased
   and to teach the elders wisdom.
23 Israel then migrated to Egypt
   and settled in the land of Ham.
24 Yahweh made the people very fruitful
   and more numerous than their oppressors.
25 whose hearts God then changed to hatred of the people
   and to conspiracy against the servants of God.
26 God chose and sent Moses and Aaron;
27 they performed signs and wonders
   in the land of Ham.
28 Yahweh sent darkness—made the land dark—
   but still they resisted God's word.
29 God turned their rivers into blood,
   killing all their fish.
30 Their country was overrun with frogs,
   even in the royal chambers;
31 God spoke: flies and mosquitoes
   swarmed through the country.
32 Yahweh sent them hail instead of rain,
   lightning flashed across their land.
33 God struck down their vines and fig trees
   and shattered the trees throughout their land.
34 Yahweh spoke: locusts came—
   grasshoppers, more than you could count—
35 eating every plant,
   every fruit their soil produced.
36 Then God struck down all the firstborn in their land,
   the entire first flowering of their fertility;
37 then God led out Israel with gold and silver,
   and not one in their tribes was left behind.
38 Egypt was happy to see them go;
   they had filled the land with dread.
39 God spread a cloud to cover them
   and fire to give them light at night.
40 They asked for food—God sent them quails
   and filled them with the bread of heaven.

41 God opened the rock—
    the waters gushed through the desert like a river.
42 Thus, faithful to the sacred promise
    given to Abraham and Sarah,
43 God led the happy people forward
    to joyful shouts from the chosen
44 and gave them the lands of the nations.
    They took possession where others had toiled,
45 on condition that they kept the statutes
    and remained obedient to God's laws.

P S A L M   1 0 6

Confession of Sin

lleluia!
1   Oh, give thanks for God is good.
    God's faithful love endures forever!
2   Who can recount the mighty deeds of God,
    or proclaim adequate praise?
3   Blessed are they who maintain justice,
    who do what is right at all times!
4   Remember me, O faithful God,
    when you show favor to your people;
    help me when you save them
5   that I may see the prosperity of your chosen ones,
    that I may rejoice in the gladness of your nation,
    that I may glory with your heritage.
6   Both we and our ancestors have sinned;
    we have committed iniquity—we have acted wickedly.
7   Our ancestors, when they were in Egypt,
    gave no thought to your wonderful works;
    they did not remember the abundance of your steadfast love,
    but rebelled against you, the Most High, at the Reed Sea.*

* The usual reading of this as "Red Sea" is based upon an ancient mistranslation.

8 Even so, you saved them as you promised,
   to make known your power.
9 You commanded the Reed Sea—and it became dry—
   then you led them through the deep water as through a desert.
10 So you, God, saved them from the hand of the foe
   and freed them from the power of the enemy.
11 The waters covered their adversaries:
   not one of them survived.
12 Then they believed God's promises;
   they sang praise.
13 But they soon forgot these deeds.
   They did not wait for God's counsel.
14 They gave way to their cravings in the wilderness
   and put God to the test in the desert.
15 God, you gave them what they asked for,
   but sent a wasting disease among them.
16 When in the camp they grew jealous
   of Moses, Miriam, and Aaron—the holy ones of God—
17 the earth opened and swallowed up Dathan
   and buried the company of Abiram.
18 Fire also broke out in their company;
   the flame burned up the wicked.
19 They made a calf in Horeb
   and worshiped a metal idol.
20 They exchanged the glory of God
   for the image of an ox that eats grass.
21 They forgot God, their Savior,
   who had done great things in Egypt,
22 wondrous deeds in the land of Ham,
   and awesome things by the Reed Sea.
23 Therefore God threatened destruction—
   but Moses and Miriam, the chosen ones,
   stood in the breach
   to turn away God's wrath from destroying them.

24 Yet they despised the pleasant land,
  having no faith in God's promise.
25 They murmured in their tents
  and did not obey the voice of God.
26 So God raised a hand and swore to them
  that they would perish in the wilderness
27 and their descendants would be dispersed among the nations,
  scattered over the lands.
28 Then they submitted themselves to the Baal of Peor
  and ate sacrifices offered to lifeless gods.
29 They provoked Yahweh to anger with their deeds,
  and a plague broke out among them.
30 Then Phinehas stood up and intervened,
  and the plague was stayed;
31 this has been reckoned to him as righteousness
  from generation to generation forever.
32 They angered God at the waters of Meribah,
  and trouble came to Moses on their account;
33 for they made Moses' spirit bitter,
  and he spoke words that were rash.
34 They did not destroy the peoples
  as God had commanded them,
35 but they mingled with the nations
  and learned their customs.
36 They served their idols,
  which became a trap to them.
37 They sacrificed their sons
  and their daughters to the demons.
38 They poured out innocent blood,
  the blood of their sons and daughters,
  whom they sacrificed to the idols of Canaan;
  and the land was polluted with blood.
39 Thus they became unclean by their acts
  and played the harlot by their deeds.
40 Then the anger of Yahweh was kindled against the people,
  and God abhorred them
41 and gave them into the hands of the nations
  so that their foes ruled over them.

42 Their enemies oppressed them
and subjected them to their power.
43 Many times, Yahweh, you delivered them,
but they were rebellious in their purposes
and were brought low through their iniquity.
44 Yet, Yahweh, you had regard for their distress
upon hearing their cry.
45 You remembered the covenant for their sake
and relented in the abundance of your great love.
46 You won compassion for your people
from those who held them captive.
47 Save us, O God,
and gather us from among the nations
that we may give thanks to your holy name
and glory in praising you.
48 Blessed be the God of Israel
from everlasting to everlasting!
Let all the people say, "Amen!"
Praise Yahweh!

P S A L M   1 0 7

God, a Refuge in All Dangers

lleluia!
1 Give thanks to Yahweh who is good,
whose love endures forever.
2 Let these be the words of Yahweh's redeemed,
those redeemed from the hands of the foe
3 by gathering them home from foreign lands,
from east and west, from north and south.
4 Some had strayed in the wilderness and the desert,
not finding a way to an inhabited town.
5 Hungry and thirsty,
their life was wasting away.

6 Then they cried to Yahweh in their anguish,
   and Yahweh rescued them from their distress,

7 guiding them by a straight road
   to a city where they could live.

8 Let them thank Yahweh for this faithful love,
   for these deeds on our behalf.

9 Satisfying the hungry,
   Yahweh fills the hungry with good things.

10 Some sat in gloom and darkness,
   prisoners suffering in chains

11 for rebeling against the orders of God,
   for scorning the counsel of the Most High.

12 God humbled them with hardship to the breaking point—
   there was no one to help them.

13 Then they cried to Yahweh in their anguish,
   and Yahweh rescued them from their distress,

14 releasing them from gloom and darkness,
   shattering their chains.

15 Let them thank Yahweh for this faithful love,
   for these wonderful deeds on our behalf—

16 breaking bronze gates open,
   bursting iron bars.

17 Some became fools through their rebellion
   and suffered affliction because of their sin.

18 Finding all food repugnant,
   they stood at death's door.

19 Then they cried to Yahweh in their anguish
   who rescued them from their distress.

20 God sent a word to heal them
   and saved them from the grave.

21 Let them thank Yahweh for this unfailing love,
   for these wonderful deeds on our behalf.

22 Let them offer thanksgiving sacrifices
   and sing with joy what Yahweh has done.

23 Those, taking ship and going to sea,
   were merchants on the waters.

24 These, too, saw what Yahweh could do,
   what wonders in the deep!

25 Yahweh spoke and raised a gale,
   lifting up towering waves.
26 Tossed to the sky, then plunged to the depths,
   they lost their courage in the ordeal,
27 staggering and reeling like drunkards
   with all their skill gone.
28 Then they cried to Yahweh in their anguish.
   Yahweh rescued them from their distress:
29 reducing the storm to a whisper
   the waves grew quiet;
30 rejoicing at the stillness,
   they landed safely at the harbor they desired.
31 Let them thank Yahweh for this faithful love,
   for these deeds on our behalf.
32 Let them laud Yahweh at the Great Assembly
   and give praise in the Council of Elders.
33 Yahweh turned rivers into desert,
   springs of water into dry ground,
34 or a fertile country into salt flats,
   because those dwelling there were evil.
35 Yahweh turned a desert into lakes,
   and a dry country into rippling brooks,
36 and gave the hungry a home—
   they built a city to dwell in.
37 There they sow the fields and plant their vineyards;
   there they have a fruitful harvest.
38 Yahweh blesses them, their numbers grow,
   and their livestock do not diminish.
39 Their numbers had fallen; they had grown weak
   through oppression, disaster, and hardship.
40 But pouring contempt upon the nobly born,
   God left them to stray in a pathless waste.
41 Yahweh raises the needy out of their misery
   and makes them numerous.
42 At the sight of this, upright hearts rejoice
   and wickedness must hold its tongue.
43 If you are wise, study these things
   and consider Yahweh's faithful love.

Prayer for Victory

1 **M**y heart is ready, O God;
  I will sing, sing your praise
and make music with all my soul.

2 Awake, lyre and harp.
  I will wake the dawn.

3 I will praise you, Yahweh, among the peoples;
  among the nations I will give thanks,

4 for your love reaches to the heavens
  and your faithfulness to the skies.

5 O God, arise above the heavens;
  may your glory be over the earth!

6 O come and deliver the ones you love—
  help us with your right hand and reply.

7 From the holy place God has made this promise:
  "I will triumph and divide the land of Shechem;
  I will measure out the valley of Succoth.

8 Gilead is mine and Manasseh.
  Ephraim I take for my helmet,
  Judah for my scepter.

9 Moab I will use for my washbowl;
  on Edom I will plant my sandal.
  Over the Philistines I will shout in triumph."

10 But who will lead me to conquer the fortified city?
   Who will bring me face to face with Edom?

11 Will you totally reject us, O God,
   and no longer march forth with us?

12 Give us help against the enemy,
   for our own power is worthless.

13 With you we shall do bravely.

An Appeal against Enemies

1 God whom I praise, speak out,
2 for now the wicked and the deceitful
are both accusing me.
They are slandering me,
3 saying malicious things about me,
attacking me without cause.
4 In return for my love, they accuse me,
though I pray for them.
5 They repay me with evil for kindness
and hatred for friendship.
6 "Appoint a wicked judge for them;
find someone to deliver the charge.
7 Let their prayer be considered a crime!
8 Let their lives be cut short;
let someone else take their offices;
9 may their children be orphaned
and their spouses widowed!
10 May their children be homeless vagabonds,
driven out of their huts;
11 may the creditor seize their possessions
and strangers grab their profits!
12 May no one show them mercy,
may no one look after their orphans,
13 may their families disappear,
their names be wiped out in one generation!
14 May the crimes of their ancestors be held against them,
and their parents' sins never be erased;
15 may Yahweh recall these constantly,
to wipe their memory off the earth!"
16 These people never thought of being kind,
but pursued the poor, the needy—
hounding the brokenhearted to death.
17 They loved cursing—let curses fall on them;
they had no taste for blessing—may it be far from them.

18 They dressed themselves in curses like garments,
   soaking right into them like water,
   sinking deep into their bones like oil.
19 Now let curses envelop them like a cloak,
   be wrapped round their waists forever.
20 May this be the payment of all my accusers from Yahweh,
   of those who speak evil against me.
21 Yahweh, defend me for the sake of your name;
   save me because your love is steadfast.
22 I am poor and weak;
   my heart is sorely tormented.
23 I am fading away like an evening shadow;
   they have shaken me off like a locust.
24 My knees are weak for lack of food;
   my body is thin for lack of oil.
25 I have become an object of mockery;
   people shake their heads at me in scorn.
26 Help me, Yahweh my God;
   save me since you love me,
27 and let them know that it is your hand—
   that it was you, Yahweh, who did it.
28 Your blessing counters their curses.
   Shame my aggressors; make your servant glad!
29 Clothe my accusers in disgrace;
   cover them with a cloak of shame.
30 I will give thanks aloud to Yahweh
   and praise God in the assembly
31 for standing at the right hand of the poor
   against those who would have sentenced them to death.

Yahweh's Oracle to You

1 **S**it at my right hand
   until I make your enemies a footstool for your feet.''
2 Yahweh, send forth your mighty scepter from Zion.
   Rule in the midst of your enemies!
3 Your people will offer themselves freely
   on the day you lead your host upon the holy mountains.
   Like dew from the womb of the dawn
   your youth will come to you.
4 Yahweh has sworn and will not retract:
   ''You are a priest forever
   after the order of Melchizedek.''
5 Yahweh is at your right hand
   and will shatter rulers on the day of wrath.
6 Yahweh will execute judgment among the nations,
   filling them with corpses,
   scattering them over the earth.
7 Yahweh will drink from the brook by the way,
   therefore strengthened and victorious!

The Great Works of God

1 **A**lleluia!
   I will thank you, Yahweh, with all my heart
   in the meeting of the just and their assembly.
2 Great are your works
   to be pondered by all who love them.
3 Glorious and sublime are your works;
   your justice stands firm forever.
4 You help us remember your wonders.
   You are compassion and love.

5   You give food to those who fear you,
    keeping your covenant ever in mind.

6   You have shown your might to your people
    by giving them the lands of the nations.

7   Your works are justice and truth;
    your precepts are all of them sure;

8   they are steadfast forever and ever,
    made in uprightness and faithfulness.

9   You have sent deliverance to your people
    and established your covenant forever.
    Holy your name, greatly to be feared.

10 To fear you is the beginning of wisdom;
    all who do so prove themselves wise.
    Your praise shall last forever!

P S A L M 1 1 2

In Praise of the Virtuous

1   Alleluia!
    Happy those who fear Yahweh
    and joyfully keep God's commandments!

2   Children of such as these will be powers on earth;
    each generation of the upright will be blessed.

3   There will be riches and wealth for their families,
    and their righteousness stands firm forever.

4   Even in the darkness, light dawns for the upright,
    for the merciful, compassionate, and righteous.

5   These good of heart lend graciously,
    handling their affairs honestly.

6   Kept safe by virtue, they are always steadfast
    and leave an everlasting memory behind them.

7   With a trusting heart and confidence in Yahweh,
    they need never fear evil news.

8   Steadfast in heart they overcome their fears;
    in the end they will triumph over their enemies.

9 Quick to be generous, they give to the poor;
their righteousness stands firm forever.
People such as these will always be honored.
10 This fills the wicked with fury
until, grinding their teeth, they waste away,
vanishing like their vain hopes.

P S A L M   1 1 3

To God the Glorious, the Merciful

1 Alleluia!
Praise, you servants of Yahweh,
praise the name of Yahweh!
2 May Yahweh's name be blessed
both now and forever!
3 From east to west, from north to south,
praised be the name of Yahweh!
4 High above all nations, Yahweh!
Your glory transcends the heavens!
5 Who is like you, Yahweh our God?
Enthroned so high, you have to stoop
6 to see the heavens and earth!
7 You raise the poor from the dust
and lift the needy from the dunghill
8 to give them a place with rulers,
with the nobles of your people.
9 Yahweh, you give the barren a home,
making them glad with children.

PSALM 114

The Wonders of the Exodus: The One True God

Alleluia!
1 When Israel came forth from Egypt,
from a foreign nation,
2 Judah became God's temple;
Israel became God's kingdom.
3 The sea fled at the sight;
the Jordan reversed its course.
4 The mountains leapt like rams,
and the hills like lambs.
5 Why was it, sea, that you fled?
Jordan, why reverse your course?
6 Mountains, why leap like rams;
hills, like lambs?
7 Tremble, O earth, before Yahweh,
in the presence of God
8 who turns the rock into a pool
and flint into a spring of water.

PSALM 115

The One True God

1 Not to us, Yahweh, not to us,
but to you alone give the glory
because of your love and your faithfulness.
2 Or some nations will say: "Where is their God?"
3 But our God is in the heavens
doing whatever God wills.
4 Their idols are silver and gold,
the work of human hands.

5 They have mouths but cannot speak;
   they have eyes but cannot see;
6 they have ears but cannot hear;
   they have nostrils but cannot smell.
7 With their hands they cannot feel;
   with their feet they cannot walk.
   No sound comes from their throats.
8 Those who make them will be like them
   and so will all who trust in them.
9 Descendants of Israel, trust in Yahweh,
   who is your help and your shield.
10 Children of Aaron, and of Miriam, trust in Yahweh,
   who is your help and your shield.
11 You who fear Yahweh, trust in Yahweh,
   who is your help and your shield.
12 Yahweh remembers us and will bless us;
   Yahweh will bless the children of Israel.
13 Yahweh will bless those who fear,
   the small and great alike.
14 May Yahweh grant increase to you,
   to you and all your children.
15 May you be blessed by Yahweh,
   the Maker of heaven and earth.
16 The heavens belong to Yahweh,
   but the earth God has given to people.
17 The dead shall not praise Yahweh,
   nor those who go down into the silence.
18 But we who live bless Yahweh
   now and forever. Amen.

Thanksgiving

1   I love you, Yahweh, because you have heard
    my voice and my supplications,
2   because you have inclined your ear to me.
    Therefore I will call on you as long as I live.
3   The cords of death encompassed me;
    the pangs of Sheol laid hold on me;
    I suffered sorrow and anguish.
4   Then I called on your name, Yahweh:
    "Oh Yahweh, I beseech you, save my life!"
5   Gracious are you, Yahweh, and righteous;
    you are full of compassion.
6   You protect the simplehearted;
    when I was brought low, you saved me.
7   Be at rest once more, O my soul,
    for Yahweh has been good to you.
8   For you, Yahweh, have delivered my soul from death,
    my eyes from tears,
    my feet from stumbling.
9   I walk before you, Yahweh,
    in the land of the living.
10 I believe even when I say,
    "I am completely crushed."
11 In my dismay I declared,
    "No one can be relied on."
12 What return can I make to Yahweh
    for all your goodness to me?
13 I will take up the cup of salvation,
    invoking the name of Yahweh.
14 I will pay what I vowed to Yahweh.
    May the whole nation be present!
15 Precious in your eyes
    is the death of your faithful.
16 Yahweh, I am your servant,
    your servant, born of a pious family;
    you have freed me from my bonds.

17 I will offer you the thanksgiving sacrifice,
    invoking your name, Yahweh.
    I will walk in your presence
    in the land of the living.
18 I will fulfill what I vowed to you
    in the presence of all the people
19 in the courts of the house of Yahweh,
    in your midst, Jerusalem.

P S A L M   1 1 7

Summons to Praise

A lleluia!
1   Praise Yahweh, all you nations;
    glorify Yahweh, all you peoples,
2 for God's love is strong,
    God's faithfulness eternal.

P S A L M   1 1 8.

Processional Hymn for the Feast of Tabernacles

A lleluia!
1   I give thanks to you, Yahweh, for you are good;
    your love is everlasting!
2 Let the house of Israel say,
    "Your love is everlasting!"
3 Let the House of Aaron say,
    "Your love is everlasting!"
4 Let those who fear Yahweh say,
    "Your love is everlasting!"

5 In desperation I called to you, Yahweh;
   you heard me and came to my aid.
6 With Yahweh at my side helping me,
   what can anyone do to me?
7 With Yahweh on my side, best help of all,
   I can triumph over my enemies.
8 I would rather take refuge in you, Yahweh,
   than rely on people;
9 I would rather take refuge in you, Yahweh,
   than rely on rulers.
10 The heathens encircled me;
   in the name of Yahweh I destroyed them.
11 They swarmed round me closer and closer;
   in the name of Yahweh I destroyed them.
12 They swarmed round me like bees;
   they flamed like a fire of thorns.
   In the name of Yahweh I destroyed them.
13 I was hard pressed, about to fall,
   but Yahweh came to my help—
14 Yahweh you are my strength and my courage.
   Yahweh, you have been my savior.
15 Let shouts of joy and victory ring out
   in the tents of the righteous;
   Yahweh's right hand has done mighty things.
16 Yahweh's right hand is lifted high.
   Yahweh's right hand has done mighty things.
17 I shall not die, but live
   to proclaim the deeds of Yahweh.
18 Though Yahweh has chastised me,
   I am not abandoned to death.
19 Open the gates of justice to me.
   I will come in and give thanks to you, Yahweh.
20 This is Yahweh's gateway,
   through which the righteous may enter.
21 I thank you for having heard me;
   you have been my savior.
22 The stone rejected by the builders
   has become the cornerstone;

23 this is Yahweh's doing,
and it is marvelous to see.
24 This is the day made memorable by Yahweh.
Let us rejoice and be glad.
25 Yahweh, please save us.
Yahweh, please help us prosper.
26 Blessings on the one who comes in the name of Yahweh!
We bless you from the house of Yahweh.
27 Yahweh is God and has made light to shine on us.
With branches in your hands, form the procession
as far as the corners of the altar.
28 You are my God, I give you thanks.
I celebrate you, my God;
I give you thanks for having heard me.
You have been my savior.
29 I give you thanks, Yahweh, for you are good;
your love is everlasting!

P S A L M   1 1 9

In Praise of God's Law

1 Happy are they whose way is blameless,
who walk according to your law.
2 Happy are they who observe your decrees,
who seek you with all their hearts.
3 They do nothing wrong
and walk in your ways.
4 You have commanded that your precepts
be faithfully obeyed.
5 I want to be firm
in keeping your statutes!
6 Then I should not be put to shame
when I behold all your commands.

7 I will give you thanks with an upright heart
   when I have learned your just ordinances.
8 I will keep your statutes.
   Do not completely abandon me.

9 How shall people be pure in their ways?
   By keeping to your words.
10 I seek you with all my heart.
   Let me not stray from your commands.
11 I treasure your promise within my heart,
   that I may not sin against you.
12 Blessed are you, Yahweh.
   Teach me your statutes.
13 With my lips I recited
   all the ordinances of your mouth.
14 I rejoice in the way of your decrees
   with joy above all wealth.
15 I will meditate on your precepts
   and concentrate on your ways.
16 I will delight in your statutes
   and never forget your words.

17 Be good to your servant
   that I may live to keep your words.
18 Open my eyes that I may marvel
   at the wonders of your law.
19 I am a pilgrim on earth.
   Show me your commands.
20 My soul is consumed with longing
   for your decrees at all times.
21 You rebuke the proud,
   the accursed who turn away from your commands.
22 Take reproach and contempt away from me,
   for I follow your decrees.
23 Though rulers connive talk against me,
   your servant meditates on your commands.
24 Yes, your decrees are my delight;
   they are my counselors.

25 I lie prostrate in the dust.
   Grant me life according to your word.
26 I confessed my ways and you answered me.
   Teach me your statutes.
27 Make me understand the way of your precepts,
   and I will meditate on your wondrous deeds.
28 My soul is weary with sorrow.
   Strengthen me according to your words.
29 Turn me from the way of falsehood
   and graciously teach me your law.
30 I have chosen the way of truth;
   I have set your law before me.
31 I hold tight to your decrees.
   Yahweh, let me not be put to shame.
32 I will run the way of your commands—
   give me strength of heart.

33 Teach me, O God, the way of your statutes
   that I may always observe them.
34 Give me discernment that I may observe your law
   and keep it with all my heart.
35 Guide me down the path of your commands,
   for I delight in it.
36 Turn my heart to your decrees
   and not to love of gain.
37 Turn my eyes away from seeing worthless things;
   by your way renew my life.
38 Fulfill your promise to your servant—
   to those who fear you.
39 Turn away from me the reproach that I dread,
   for your edicts are good.
40 See, I long for your precepts;
   in your justice, give me life.

41 Let your steadfast love come to me, O God,
   your salvation according to your promise.
42 So shall I have an answer for those who reproach me,
   for I trust in your words.

43 Leave the word of truth in my mouth—
   for in your decree is my hope—
44 and I will keep your law continually,
   forever and ever.
45 I will walk the open road
   because I seek your precepts.
46 I will speak of your decrees before nobles
   without being ashamed;
47 and I will delight in your commands,
   which I love.
48 I will lift up my hands to your commands
   and meditate on your statutes.

49 Remember your word to your servant
   since you have given me hope.
50 My comfort in my affliction is
   that your promise gives me life.
51 Though the proud mock me bitterly,
   I have not deviated from your law.
52 I remember your judgments of old, O God,
   and I am comforted.
53 Indignation seizes me
   because of the wicked who forsake your law.
54 Your decrees are my song
   in the place of my exile.
55 By night I remember your name, O God.
   I will keep your law.
56 This is my blessing:
   that I have observed your precepts.

57 I have said, O God,
   that my lot is to keep your words.
58 I entreat you with all my heart:
   have pity on me according to your promise.
59 I thought about my ways
   and turned my steps to your decrees.
60 I was prompt and hastened
   to keep your commands.

61 Though the snares of the wicked are twined about me,
    I have not forgotten your law.
62 At midnight I rise to give you thanks
    because of your just ordinances.
63 I am the friend of all who fear you
    and keep your precepts.
64 Of your kindness, O God, the earth is full.
    Teach me your statutes.

65 You have done good to your servant,
    O God, according to your word.
66 Teach me wisdom and knowledge,
    for I trust in your commands.
67 Before I was tried I went astray,
    but now I hold to your promise.
68 You are good and gracious.
    Teach me your law.
69 Though the proud spread lies about me,
    with all my heart I will observe your precepts.
70 Their heart has become callous and unfeeling:
    as for me, your law is my delight.
71 It is good for me to be afflicted,
    that I may learn your decrees.
72 Your law is more precious to me
    than thousands of gold and silver pieces.

73 Your hands have made me and fashioned me.
    Give me discernment that I may learn your commands.
74 Those who fear you will watch me and be glad
    because I hope in your word.
75 I know, O God, that your edicts are just,
    and you have rightly afflicted me.
76 Let your steadfast love console me
    according to the promise to your servants.
77 Let your compassion come to me that I may live,
    for your law is my delight.
78 Let the proud be put to shame for oppressing me unjustly;
    but as for me, I will meditate on your precepts.

79 Let those who fear you turn to me
and acknowledge your decrees.
80 Let my heart be blameless in your statutes
that I may not be put to shame.

81 My soul longs for your salvation;
I hope in your word.
82 My eyes ache after your promise.
When will you comfort me?
83 Though I am shriveled like a wineskin in the smoke,
I have not forgotten your decrees.
84 How many are the days of your servant?
When will you judge my persecutors?
85 The proud have dug pits for me,
contrary to your law.
86 All your commands are trustworthy;
help me when they persecute me unfairly.
87 They have almost put an end to me on the earth,
but I have not forsaken your precepts.
88 In your steadfast love give me life
that I may keep the mandates of your mouth.

89 Your word, O God, endures forever;
it stands firm as heaven.
90 Through all generations your truth endures;
you have established the earth, and it stands firm.
91 By your decree it endures to this day,
for all things serve you.
92 Had not your law been my delight,
I should have perished in my affliction.
93 I will never forget your precepts,
for through them you give me life.
94 I am yours. Save me,
for I seek your precepts.
95 The wicked wait to destroy me,
but I ponder your decrees.
96 I see that all fulfillment has its limits,
but broad indeed is your command.

97 How I love your law, O God!
   I think of it all the day.
98 Your commandments make me wiser than my enemies,
   for they are ever with me.
99 I understand more than all my teachers
   when your law is my meditation.
100 I have more discernment than the elders
   because I observe your precepts.
101 From every evil way I have kept my feet
   so that I may obey your words.
102 From your decrees I have not swerved,
   for you have taught me.
103 How sweet to my palate are your promises—
   sweeter than honey to my mouth!
104 I gain discernment through your precepts;
   therefore I hate every falsehood.

105 Your word is a lamp for my steps,
   a light to my path.
106 I resolve and have taken an oath
   to follow your just decrees.
107 I am sorely afflicted.
   Give me life according to your word.
108 Accept the willing praise of my mouth, O God,
   and teach me your decrees.
109 Though I constantly take my life in my hands,
   I will not forget your law.
110 The wicked have laid a snare for me,
   but from your precepts I have not wandered.
111 Your decrees are my inheritance forever;
   they are the joy of my heart.
112 My heart is set on keeping your statutes
   to the end.

113 I hate those of divided heart,
   but I love your law.
114 You are my refuge, my shield;
   I hope in your word.

115 Leave me, you wrongdoers,
that I may keep the commands of my God.
116 As you have promised—
sustain me that I may live;
disappoint me not in my hope.
117 Help me, that I may be safe
and ever delight in your decrees.
118 You despise all who stray from your statutes,
for their deceitfulness is in vain.
119 You account all the wicked of the earth as dung;
therefore I love your decrees.
120 My flesh trembles in fear of you,
and I stand in awe of your law.

121 I have done what is just and right;
do not give me to my oppressors.
122 Ensure the well-being of your servant;
do not let the proud oppress me.
123 My eyes ache, seeking for salvation
and your promise of justice.
124 Deal with your servant according to your steadfast love,
and teach me your statutes.
125 I am your servant.
Guide me that I may know your mandates.
126 Yahweh, now is the time for you to act.
They have broken your law.
127 For I love your commandments
more than gold, however fine.
128 In all your precepts I go forward;
every false way I hate.

129 Wonderful are your sayings;
therefore I observe them.
130 The revelation of your words sheds light,
giving understanding to the simple.
131 I open my mouth and sigh
in my yearning for your commands.
132 Turn to me in pity
as you turn to those who love your name.

133 Free my footsteps according to your promise
and let no evil rule over me.
134 Redeem me from oppression
that I may keep your precepts.
135 Let your face shine upon your servant,
and teach me your statutes.
136 My eyes shed streams of tears
because your law has not been kept.

137 You are just, O God,
and your law is right.
138 You have imposed your decrees in justice
and in perfect constancy.
139 My zeal consumes me
because my foes ignore your words.
140 Your promise is well-tested,
and your servant loves it.
141 I am weak and despised,
but I have not forgotten your precepts.
142 Your justice is everlasting,
and your law is permanent.
143 Though distress and anguish have come over me,
your commands are my delight.
144 Your decrees are always just.
Give me discernment that I may live.

145 I cry out with my heart. Answer me, O God.
I will observe your statutes.
146 I call upon you. Save me
and I will keep your decrees.
147 In the first light, I rise and cry out;
I hope in your words.
148 My eyes greet the night
in meditation on your promise.
149 Hear my voice according to your steadfast love, O God;
preserve my life according to your justice.
150 I am attacked by malicious persecutors
who are far from your law.

151 You, O God, are near,
  and all your commands are true.
152 Long ago I learned from your decrees
  that you have established them forever.

153 Note my suffering and save me,
  for I have not forgotten your law.
154 Defend my cause and redeem me;
  for the sake of your promise give me life.
155 Salvation is far from sinners
  because they do not seek your statutes.
156 Your compassion is great, O God;
  renew my life according to your justice.
157 Though my persecutors and my foes are many,
  I do not turn away from your decrees.
158 I looked on the faithless with disgust,
  because they do not guard your promise.
159 See how I love your law, O God;
  in your steadfast love give me life.
160 All of your words are true;
  each of your just decrees is eternal.

161 Rulers torment me without cause,
  but my heart stands in awe of your word.
162 I rejoice at your promise
  as one who has found a great treasure.
163 Falsehood I reject and abhor;
  but your law I love.
164 I praise you seven times a day
  for your just decrees.
165 Those who love your law have great peace,
  and for them there is no stumbling block.
166 I wait for your salvation, O God,
  and I fulfill your commands.
167 I keep your decrees
  and love them deeply.
168 I keep your precepts and your decrees,
  for all my ways are in your sight.

169 Let my cry come before you, O God;
in keeping your word, give me understanding.

170 May my supplication reach you;
deliver me according to your promise.

171 My lips pour forth your praise
because you teach me your statutes.

172 My tongue sings of your promise,
for all your commandments are just.

173 Let your hand be ready to help me,
for I have chosen your precepts.

174 I long for your salvation, O God,
and your law is my delight.

175 Let my soul live and praise you,
and may your laws help me.

176 I have wandered astray like a lost sheep;
O seek your servant
because I do not forget your commands.

P S A L M   1 2 0

The Enemies of Peace

1 When I was in trouble I called to you, Yahweh,
and you answered me.

2 Save me from liars and deceivers!

3 You liars, what will God do to you?
How will God punish you?

4 With a soldier's sharp arrows,
with burning coals!

5 Living among you is as bad as living in Meshech,
or among the people of Kedar!

6 Too long I have lived
with people who hate peace!

7 When I speak of peace,
they are for war.

PSALM 121

The Guardian of Israel

1 **I** lift my eyes to the mountains.
  Where is help to come from?
2 My help comes from Yahweh,
  who made heaven and earth.
3 Yahweh does not let our footsteps slip!
  Our guard does not sleep!
4 The guardian of Israel
  does not slumber or sleep.
5 Yahweh guards you, shades you.
  With Yahweh at your right hand
6 the sun cannot harm you by day
  nor the moon at night.
7 Yahweh guards you from harm,
  protects your lives;
8 Yahweh watches over your coming and going,
  now and for always.

PSALM 122

Hail, Jerusalem

1 **I** rejoiced when they said to me,
  "Let us go to the house of Yahweh!"
2 And now our feet are standing
  within your gates, O Jerusalem.
3 Jerusalem restored!
  The city, united and whole!
4 Here the tribes come up,
  the tribes of Yahweh;
  they come to praise Yahweh's name,
  according to the decree given to Israel.

5 Here are the tribunals of justice,
  the royal throne of David.
6 Pray for peace in Jerusalem:
  "Security to your houses!
7 Peace inside your city walls!
  Security to your towers!"
8 Since all are my neighbors and friends,
  I say, "Peace be with you!"
9 Since Yahweh our God lives here,
  I pray for your good.

P S A L M   1 2 3

Cry for Help: A Pilgrimage Song

1 To you have I lifted up my eyes,
  you who dwell in the heavens.
2 Behold, like the eyes of slaves
  are on the hand of their master,
  like the eyes of servants
  on the hand of their mistress,
3 so our eyes are on you, Yahweh our God,
  till you show us your mercy.
4 Have mercy on us, Yahweh! Have mercy!
  We have endured much contempt.
5 Indeed, all too full is our soul
  with scorn from the rich,
  with scorn from the proud.

God, the Savior of the People

1 **W**hat if Yahweh had not been on our side?
   Answer, Israel!
2 "If Yahweh had not been on our side
   when our enemies attacked us,
3 then they would have swallowed us alive
   in their furious anger against us.
4 Then the flood would have carried us away;
   the water would have engulfed us—
5 the raging torrent would have swept over us."
6 Let us praise Yahweh,
   who has not let our enemies destroy us.
7 We have escaped like a bird from the hunter's trap;
   the trap has been broken and we are free!
8 Our help comes from Yahweh,
   the Maker of heaven and earth.

PSALM 125

God, the Protector of the Faithful

1 **T**hose who trust in you, Yahweh, are like Mount Zion,
   which cannot be moved, but endures forever.
2 As the mountains are round about Jerusalem,
   so you are round about your people
   both now and forevermore.
3 For the scepter of wickedness shall not rest
   upon the land allotted to the righteous,
   lest the just put forth their hands to do wrong.
4 Do good, Yahweh, to those who are good,
   and to those who are upright in their hearts!
5 But those who turn aside to crooked ways
   you will lead away with evildoers!
   Peace be in Israel!

P S A L M 1 2 6

Song of the Returning Exiles

1 **W**hen God brought back the captives of Zion,
we were like those who dream.
2 Then our mouths were filled with laughter
and our tongues with rejoicing;
then they said among the nations,
"Yahweh has done great things for them."
3 Yahweh has done great things for us;
we are truly glad.
4 Restore our fortunes, Yahweh,
like the streams in the Negeb!
5 May those who sow in tears
reap with songs of joy!
6 Those that go forth weeping,
carrying the seed for sowing,
shall come home with shouts of joy,
bringing the sheaves with them.

P S A L M 1 2 7

Trust in Providence

1 **I**f Yahweh does not build the house,
in vain do the builders toil;
if Yahweh does not guard the city,
in vain do the sentries watch.
2 In vain you rise early
and delay going to bed,
toiling to make a living,
since Yahweh provides for the beloved as they sleep.
3 Children are a gift from Yahweh,
who rewards with descendants;

4 like the arrow in a victor's hand
are your children.
5 Happy those who have filled their quivers
with arrows of this sort;
they will not be put to shame,
in disputes with their enemies at the gate.

P S A L M   1 2 8

The Blessings of Home: A Pilgrimage Song

1 O blessed are you who fear Yahweh
and walk in God's ways!
2 You will eat the fruit of your labor.
Happy shall you be and prosperous.
3 You will be like a fruitful vine within your house,
your children like shoots of the olive around your table.
4 Indeed thus shall one be blessed
who fears Yahweh.
5 May Yahweh bless you from Zion
all the days of your life!
6 May you see your children's children
in a happy Jerusalem!
Peace be upon Israel.

Prayer for the Overthrow of Israel's Foes

1 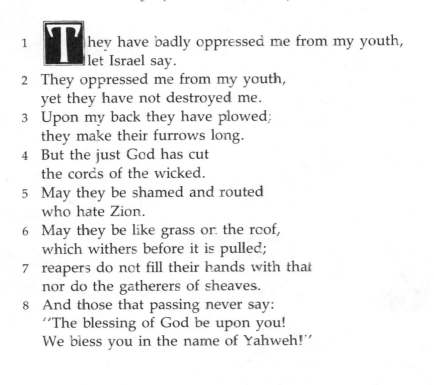They have badly oppressed me from my youth,
let Israel say.
2 They oppressed me from my youth,
yet they have not destroyed me.
3 Upon my back they have plowed;
they make their furrows long.
4 But the just God has cut
the cords of the wicked.
5 May they be shamed and routed
who hate Zion.
6 May they be like grass on the roof,
which withers before it is pulled;
7 reapers do not fill their hands with that
nor do the gatherers of sheaves.
8 And those that passing never say:
"The blessing of God be upon you!
We bless you in the name of Yahweh!"

P S A L M   1 3 0

Prayer for Pardon and Mercy

1 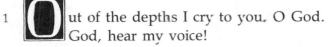Out of the depths I cry to you, O God.
God, hear my voice!
2 Let your ears be attentive
to my cry for mercy.
3 If you, O God, mark our guilt,
who can stand?
4 But with you is forgiveness;
and for this we revere you.

5 I trust in you, O God,
  my soul trusts in your word.
6 My soul waits for you, O God.
  More than sentinels wait for the dawn,
  let Israel wait for you.
7 For with you is faithful love
  and plentiful redemption.
8 You will redeem Israel
  from all their iniquities.

P S A L M   1 3 1

Childlike Trust in God

1 Yahweh, my heart has no false pride;
  my eyes do not look too high.
  I am not concerned with great affairs
  or things far above me.
2 It is enough for me to keep my soul still and quiet
  like a child in its mother's arms,
  as content as a child that has been weaned.
3 Israel, hope in Yahweh,
  now and for always!

God's Promise to David: A Pilgrimage Song

1 O God, remember David
and all the many hardships he endured,
2 the oath he swore to Yahweh,
his vow to the Mighty One of Jacob.
3 I will not enter my house
or go to the bed where I rest.
4 I will give no sleep to my eyes;
to my eyelids I will give no slumber
5 until I find a place for God,
a dwelling for the Mighty One of Israel.
6 At Ephrata we heard of the ark;
we found it in the plains of Yearim.
7 Let us go to the place of God's dwelling;
let us worship at Yahweh's footstool.
8 Arise, Yahweh, and come to the place of your rest,
you and the ark of your strength.
9 Your priests shall be clothed with justice;
your faithful shall shout their joy.
10 For the sake of David your servant,
do not reject your anointed.
11 Yahweh swore an oath to David
and will not go back on this word:
"An offspring, the fruit of your body
I will set upon your throne.
12 If they keep my covenant in truth
and my laws that I have taught them,
then their descendants shall rule
on your throne from age to age."
13 For Yahweh has chosen Zion
and prefers it for a dwelling:
14 "This is my resting-place forever,
here I have chosen to live.
15 I will bless it with abundant produce;
I will fill the poor with bread.

16 I will clothe Zion's priests with salvation,
   and the faithful shall ring out their joy.
17 Here David's stock will flower;
   I will place a lamp for my anointed.
18 I will cover their enemies with shame,
   but on them my crown shall shine."

P S A L M   1 3 3

In Praise of Love

1 How good it is, how pleasant,
   for God's people to live in unity.
2 It is like the precious oil
   running down from Aaron's head and beard,
   down to the collar of his robes.
3 It is like the dew on Mount Hermon
   falling on the hills of Zion.
   For there Yahweh has promised a blessing,
   life that never ends.

P S A L M   1 3 4

Night Hymn

1 Come, bless Yahweh,
   all you who serve Yahweh,
   ministering in the house of Yahweh,
   in the courts of the house of our God!
2 Lift up your hands toward the sanctuary;
   praise Yahweh night after night!
3 May Yahweh bless you from Zion,
   the One who made heaven and earth!

Anthology of Praise

1 Alleluia!
   Praise the name of Yahweh;
   praise God, you servants of Yahweh

2 who stand in the house of Yahweh,
   minister in the courts of the house of our God.

3 Praise Yahweh, who is good.
   Sing praise to God, who is loving;

4 for Yahweh has chosen Israel
   for a treasured possession.

5 I know Yahweh is great,
   that our God is greater than all gods.

6 Yahweh's will is done in heaven, on earth,
   and in the depths of the seas.

7 Yahweh summons clouds from the ends of the earth,
   sends lightning with the rain;
   from the storehouse Yahweh sends forth the wind.

8 Yahweh struck down the firstborn of the Egyptians,
   human and beast alike.

9 Yahweh worked signs and wonders
   in your midst, O Egypt,
   against Pharaoh and all his servants.

10 Yahweh struck down nations in their greatness,
    and God slew mighty rulers:

11 Sihon, king of the Amorites,
    Og, the king of Bashan,
    and all the kings of Canaan.

12 Yahweh gave Israel their land as an inheritance,
    an inheritance for God's people.

13 Yahweh, your name stands forever,
    remembered from age to age—

14 for you do justice for your people.
    You have compassion on your servants.

15 The idols of the nations are silver and gold,
    the work of human hands.

16   They have mouths but they cannot speak;
     eyes but they cannot see.

17   They have ears but cannot hear;
     nor is there breath on their lips.

18   Their makers will come to be like them,
     and so will all who trust in them!

19   Descendants of Israel, bless Yahweh!
     Children of Aaron and Miriam, bless Yahweh.

20   House of Levi, bless Yahweh!
     You who fear Yahweh, bless our God.

21   From Zion may Yahweh be blessed,
     the God who dwells in Jerusalem!

PSALM 136

Litany of Thanksgiving

Alleluia!

1 We give thanks to you, Yahweh, for you are good.
   Your love is everlasting!

2 We give thanks to you, God of gods.
   Your love is everlasting!

3 You alone do great wonders.
   Your love is everlasting!

4 Your wisdom made the heavens.
   Your love is everlasting!

5 You spread out the earth on the waters.
   Your love is everlasting!

6 You made the great lights.
   Your love is everlasting!

7 The sun to rule the day.
   Your love is everlasting!

8 Moon and stars to rule the night.
   Your love is everlasting!

9 You struck down the firstborn of Egypt.
   Your love is everlasting!

10 And brought Israel out from among them.
    Your love is everlasting!
11 With a mighty hand and outstretched arm.
    Your love is everlasting!
12 You split the Sea of Reeds.
    Your love is everlasting!
13 Led Israel through the midst of it.
    Your love is everlasting!
14 Drowned Pharaoh and his army.
    Your love is everlasting!
15 You led your people through the wilderness.
    Your love is everlasting!
16 You struck down mighty rulers.
    Your love is everlasting!
17 You slaughtered famous kings.
    Your love is everlasting!
18 Sihon, king of the Amorites
    Your love is everlasting!
19 And Og, the king of Bashan.
    Your love is everlasting!
20 You gave their lands as an inheritance.
    Your love is everlasting!
21 An inheritance to your servant Israel.
    Your love is everlasting!
22 You remembered us when we were down.
    Your love is everlasting!
23 And freed us from our oppressors.
    Your love is everlasting!
24 You provide for all living creatures.
    Your love is everlasting!
25 Give thanks to the God of Heaven,
    for God's love is everlasting!

The Exile's Remembrance of Zion

1   **B**y the rivers of Babylon
    we sat and wept, remembering Zion.
2   On the poplars of that land
    we hung up our harps;
3   there our captors asked of us
    the lyrics of our songs
    and urged us to be joyous:
    "Sing for us one of the songs of Zion!" they said.
4   How could we sing a song of Yahweh
    while in a foreign land?
5   If I forget you, Jerusalem,
    may my right hand forget its skill!
6   May my tongue cleave to the roof of my mouth
    if I forget you,
    if I do not consider Jerusalem
    my greatest joy.
7   Remember, Yahweh, what the Edomites did
    that day in Jerusalem.
    When they said "Tear it down,
    tear it down to its foundations!"
8   O daughter of Babylon—you destroyer—
    happy those who shall repay you
    the evil you have done us!
9   Happy those who shall seize and smash
    your little ones against the rock!

A Prayer of Thanksgiving

1   I thank you, Yahweh, with all my heart;
    I sing praise to you before the angels.
2   I worship at your holy temple and praise your name
    because of your constant love and faithfulness,
    because you have shown that you and your word are exalted.
3   You answered me when I called to you;
    you built up strength within me.
4   All the rulers of the earth will praise you, Yahweh,
    because they have heard your promises.
5   They will sing about your ways
    and about your great glory.
6   Even though you are exalted,
    you care for the lowly.
    The proud cannot hide from you.
7   Even when I am surrounded by troubles,
    you keep me safe;
    you oppose my angry enemies
    and save me by your power.
8   You will do everything you have promised me;
    Yahweh, your faithful love endures forever.
    Complete the work that you have begun.

In Praise of God's Omniscience

1 **Y**ahweh, you search me and know me.
2 You know if I am standing or sitting.
  You perceive my thoughts from far away.
3 Whether I walk or lie down, you are watching;
  you are familiar with all my ways.
4 Before a word is even on my tongue, Yahweh,
  you know it completely.
5 Close behind and close in front you hem me in,
  shielding me with your hand.
6 Such knowledge is beyond my understanding,
  too high beyond my reach.
7 Where could I go to escape your spirit?
  Where could I flee from your presence?
8 If I climb to the heavens, you are there;
  there, too, if I sink to Sheol.
9 If I flew to the point of sunrise—
  or far across the sea—
10 your hand would still be guiding me,
  your right hand holding me.
11 If I asked darkness to cover me
  and light to become night around me,
12 that darkness would not be dark to you;
  night would shine as the day.
13 You created my inmost being
  and knit me together in my mother's womb.
14 For all these mysteries—
  for the wonder of myself,
  for the wonder of your works—
  I thank you.
15 You know me through and through
  from having watched my bones take shape
  when I was being formed in secret,
  woven together in the womb.

16 You have seen my every action;
all were recorded in your book—
my days determined
17 even before the first one began.
God, your thoughts are mysterious!
How vast is their sum.
18 I could no more count them
than I could count the sand!
And even if I could,
you would still be with me.
19 God, if only you would destroy the wicked!
20 They speak evil about you,
regard your thoughts as nothing.
21 Yahweh, I hate those who hate you
and loathe those who rise against you.
22 I hate them with a total hatred;
they are my enemies, too.
23 God, search me and know my heart;
probe me and know my thoughts.
24 Make sure I do not follow evil ways,
and guide me in the way of life eternal.

P S A L M   1 4 0

Deliverance

1 Deliver me, O God, from evil people;
preserve me from the violent,
2 from those who plan evil things in their hearts
and stir up wars every day.
3 They make their tongues as sharp as serpents',
and on their lips is the poison of vipers.
4 Save me, O God, from the wiles of the wicked;
protect me from the violent,
who have planned to trip up my feet.

5 The proud have hidden a trap for me,
and with cords they have spread a net.
By the path they have set snares for me.
6 I say, "You are my God.
Give ear to my cry for mercy."
7 O God, my God, my strong deliverer,
you have shielded my head in the day of battle.
8 Grant not, O God, the desires of the wicked;
do not let their evil plot succeed.
9 Those who surround me proudly hold up their heads.
Let the mischief of their lips overwhelm them!
10 Let burning coals fall upon them!
Let them be cast into the fire, no more to rise!
11 Let the slanderer be driven from the land;
quickly let disaster hunt down the violent!
12 I know that God secures justice for the poor
and upholds the cause of the needy.
13 Surely the just shall give thanks to your name;
the upright shall dwell in your presence.

P S A L M   1 4 1

Against the Attractions of Evil

1 Yahweh, I am calling. Hasten to me;
hear me—I am calling to you.
2 My prayers rise like incense,
my hands like the evening sacrifice.
3 Yahweh, set a guard at my mouth,
a watch at the door of my lips.
4 Do not let my heart be compelled to wrong doing,
to share in the deeds of the evildoers.
No, I will not taste their delights.

5 A just person may strike me in reproof—
it is a kindness;
such a rebuke is oil on my head!
My prayer is ever against the deeds of evildoers.
6 When their judges are flung into a crag,
they will learn just how pleasant my words have been.
7 "Like a millstone smashed on the ground,
our bones are scattered at the mouth of Sheol."
8 To you, Yahweh, I turn my eyes.
In you I take shelter—
do not hand me over to death.
9 Keep me out of traps that are set for me,
from the bait laid for me by evil ones.
10 Let the wicked fall into their own net
while I pass by in safety.

P S A L M   1 4 2

Prayer of One Deserted by Friends

1 **W**ith all my voice I cry to you, Yahweh;
with all my voice I entreat you.
2 I pour out my complaint before you;
I tell you all my distress.
3 When my spirit faints within me,
you, Yahweh, know my path.
On the way where I shall walk
they have hidden a snare to trap me.
4 I look on my right and see:
there is no one who takes my part.
I have lost all means of escape,
there is no one who cares for my life.

5 I cry to you, Yahweh,
   I have said: "You are my refuge,
   all I have in the land of the living."
6 Listen, then, to my cry,
   for I am in the depths of distress.
   Rescue me from those who pursue me,
   for they are too strong for me.
7 Bring my soul out of this prison,
   and then I shall praise your name.
   Around me the just will gather
   because of your goodness to me.

P S A L M   1 4 3

A Prayer for Help

1 **G**od, hear my prayer.
   Listen to my plea!
   You are just and faithful—
   so answer me!
2 Do not put me, your servant, on trial,
   for no one is innocent in your sight.
3 My enemy has pursued me
   and completely defeated me.
   My foe has put me in a dark prison,
   and I am like those long dead.
4 So my spirit grows faint within me,
   I am in deep despair.
5 I remember the days of old:
   I ponder all that you have done;
   I bring to mind all your deeds.
6 I stretch out my hands to you in prayer;
   like dry ground my soul thirsts for you.

7 Answer me now, O God.
   I have lost all hope!
   Do not hide your face from me,
   or I will be among those who go down to the land of the dead.
8 I trust in you—
   at dawn remind me of your faithful love.
   To you I lift my soul;
   show me the way I should go.
9 I look to you for protection, O God.
   Rescue me from my enemies.
10 You are my God—
   teach me to do your will.
   May your good spirit
   guide me on a safe path.
11 Save me, O God, as you have promised;
   in your justice rescue me from my troubles!
12 In your faithful love for me, protect me
   because I am your servant.

P S A L M   1 4 4

Prayer for Victory and Prosperity

1 **B**lessed be you, O God, my Rock,
   who trains my hands for battle,
   my arms for struggle;
2 my Refuge and my Fortress,
   my Stronghold, my Deliverer,
   my Shield in whom I trust.
3 God, what are we, that you care for us
   or even take thought of us?
4 We are like a breath,
   our days, like a passing shadow.
5 Part your heavens, O God, and come down;
   touch the mountains and they shall smoke.

6 Send forth lightning, and put them to flight;
  shoot your arrows and rout them.
7 Reach out your hand from on high—
  rescue me from the mighty waters,
  from the hands of strangers,
8 whose mouths swear false promises
  while their right hands are raised in perjury.
9 O God, I will sing a new song to you;
  with a ten-stringed lyre I will sing your praise—
10 you who give victory to rulers
  and deliver David, your servant.
11 From the evil sword deliver me;
  and rescue me from the hands of strangers
  whose mouths swear false promises
  while their right hands are raised in perjury.
12 May our children be like plants
  well-nurtured in their youth,
  our descendants like wrought columns
  such as stand at the corners of the temple.
13 May our barns be full,
  with every kind of crop;
  may our sheep be in the thousands
  and increase to myriads in our fields.
  May our oxen be strong.
14 May there be no breach in our walls, no exile,
  no outcry in our streets.
15 Happy the people for whom this is true;
  happy the people whose God is Yahweh.

The Greatness and Goodness of God

1 I sing your praises, O my God,
and I will praise your name forever and ever.

2 Every day will I bless you,
and I will praise your name forever and ever.

3 Great are you, Yahweh, and most worthy of praise;
your greatness is beyond our understanding.

4 Generation after generation
praises your work and proclaims your might.

5 They speak of your splendor and glorious renown
and proclaim your wondrous works.

6 They discourse on the power of your wonderful deeds
and declare your greatness.

7 They publish the fame of your abundant goodness
and joyfully sing of your justice.

8 Yahweh, you are gracious and compassionate,
slow to anger and full of love.

9 Yahweh, you are good to all
and have compassion on all your works.

10 All your works give you thanks, O God,
and your faithful ones bless you.

11 They discourse on the glory of your reign
and speak of your might.

12 May humankind learn of your power
and the glorious splendor of your reign.

13 Your reign is a reign for all ages,
and your dominion endures for all generations.
Yahweh, you are faithful in all your words
and holy in all your works.

14 You lift up all who are falling
and raise up all who are bowed down.

15 The eyes of all look hopefully to you,
and you give them bread in due season.

16 You open your hand
and satisfy the desire of every living thing.

17 Yahweh, you are just in all your ways
and loving in all your works.

18 You are near to all who call upon you,
to all who call upon you sincerely.

19 You fulfill the desire of those who fear you,
you hear their cry and save them.

20 You watch over all who love you,
but all the wicked you will destroy.

21 May my mouth speak your praise, Yahweh,
and may all creatures bless your holy name forever and ever.

P S A L M   1 4 6

Trust in God Alone

1 **A**lleluia!
Praise Yahweh, O my soul!

2 I will praise, you, Yahweh, all my life;
I will sing praise to you as long as I live.

3 Do not put your trust in rulers,
in humans in whom there is no salvation.

4 When their spirits depart they return to the earth;
on that very day their plans perish.

5 Happy those whose help is the God of Jacob and Rachel,
whose hope is in Yahweh, their God,

6 the Maker of heaven and earth,
the sea, and all that is in them;

7 who keeps faith forever,
secures justice for the oppressed,
and gives food to the hungry.

8 Yahweh, you set captives free
and give sight to the blind.
You raise up those that were bowed down
and love the just.

9   You protect strangers;
      the orphan and the widow you sustain,
      but the way of the wicked you thwart.
10 Yahweh shall reign forever—
      your God, O Zion, through all generations. Alleluia.

P S A L M   1 4 7

Zion's Grateful Praise to a Bountiful God

1   **P**raise God, who is good;
      sing praise to our God, who is gracious.
      It is fitting to praise God.
2   God rebuilds Jerusalem,
      gathers the exiles of Israel.
3   God heals the brokenhearted
      and binds up all their wounds.
4   God knows the number of the stars
      and calls them each by name.
5   Great is our God and mighty in power;
      there is no limit to God's wisdom.
6   Yahweh sustains the lowly
      and casts the wicked to the ground.
7   Sing to God with thanksgiving;
      sing praise with the harp to our God,
8   who covers the heavens with clouds,
      who provides rain for the earth,
      and who makes grass grow on the mountains,
9   who gives food to the cattle,
      and to the young ravens when they call.
10 God does not delight in the strength of the steed,
      nor is God pleased with the fleetness of humans.
11 God is pleased with those who have reverence,
      with those who hope in faithful love.

12 Glorify Yahweh, O Jerusalem;
   praise your God, O Zion.
13 For God has strengthened the bars of your gates
   and has blessed your children within you.
14 God has granted peace on your borders
   and fills you with the best of wheat.
15 God sends forth a command to the earth;
   swiftly runs the word!
16 God spreads snow like wool
   and scatters frost like ashes.
17 God scatters hail like crumbs;
   before God's cold, the waters freeze.
18 God sends a word and melts them;
   God lets the breeze blow and the waters flow.
19 God's word has been proclaimed to Jacob,
   laws and decrees to Israel.
20 God has not done this for any other nation;
   God has not made such laws known to them. Alleluia.

P S A L M   1 4 8

Hymn of All Creation to the Creator

1 Praise God from the heavens;
   praise God in the heights;
2 praise God, all you angels;
   praise God, all you heavenly hosts.
3 Praise God, sun and moon;
   praise God, all you shining stars.
4 Praise God, you highest heavens,
   and you waters above the heavens.

5 Let them praise the name of God,
   who commanded and they were created.
6 God established them forever and ever
   and gave a decree which shall not pass away.
7 Praise God all the earth,
   you sea monsters and all depths,
8 fire and hail, snow and mist,
   storm winds that fulfill God's word.
9 You mountains and all you hills,
   you fruit trees and all you cedars,
10 you wild beasts and all tame animals,
   you creeping things and flying birds.
11 Let the rulers of the earth and all peoples
   and all the judges of the earth—
12 young men too, and maidens,
   old women and men—
13 praise the name of God
   whose name alone is exalted;
   whose majesty is above earth and heaven,
   and who has raised the fortunes of the people.
14 Be this God praised by all the faithful ones,
   by the children of Israel, the people close to God.
   Alleluia.

P S A L M   1 4 9

Invitation to Glorify God with Song

1 **S**ing to Yahweh a new song of praise
   in the assembly of the faithful.
2 Let Israel rejoice in their Maker;
   let the people of Zion be glad in their God.
3 Let them praise God's name in a festive dance;
   let them sing praise to God with timbrel and harp.
4 For God loves the people
   and crowns the lowly with victory.

5 Let the faithful rejoice;
   let them sing for joy upon their couches—
6 let the high praises of God be in their mouths.
   And let two-edged swords be in their hands
7 to execute vengeance on the nations,
   punishments on the peoples;
8 to bind their rulers with chains,
   their nobles with fetters;
9 to execute on them the written sentence.
   This is the glory of all the faithful.
   Alleluia.

P S A L M 1 5 0

Final Doxology with Full Orchestra

1 Alleluia!
   Praise to you, Yahweh, in your sanctuary!
   Praise to you in the firmament of your strength.
2 Praise you for your mighty deeds;
   praise you for your sovereign majesty.
3 Praise to you, Yahweh, with the blast of the trumpet,
   praise with lyre and harp.
4 Praise with timbrel and dance;
   praise with strings and flute.
5 Praise to you, Yahweh, with resounding cymbals;
   praise with clanging cymbals.
6 Let everything that has breath praise Yahweh.
   Alleluia.